Planning and Managing Death Issues in the Schools

PLANNING AND MANAGING DEATH ISSUES IN THE SCHOOLS

A HANDBOOK

Robert L. Deaton
and
William A. Berkan

The Greenwood Educators' Reference Collection

GREENWOOD PRESS
Westport, Connecticut • London

Library of Congress Cataloging-in-Publication Data

Deaton, Bob.
　　Planning and managing death issues in the schools : a handbook /
Robert L. Deaton and William A. Berkan.
　　　　p.　cm.—(The Greenwood educators' reference collection,
ISSN 1056–2192
　　　Includes bibliographical references and index.
　　　ISBN 0–313–29525–5 (alk. paper)
　　　　1. Children and death.　2. Bereavement in children.　3. Children—
Death—Psychological aspects.　4. Death—Study and teaching.
　　　5. Bereavement—Psychological aspects—Study and teaching.
　　　I. Berkan, William A.　II. Title.
　　BF723.D3D44　1995
　　362.2—dc20　　　　　94–21693

British Library Cataloguing in Publication Data is available.

Library of Congress Catalog Card Number: 94–21693
ISBN: 0–313–29525–5
ISSN: 1056–2192

First published in 1995

Greenwood Press, 88 Post Road West, Westport, CT 06881
An imprint of Greenwood Publishing Group, Inc.

Printed in the United States of America

The paper used in this book complies with the
Permanent Paper Standard issued by the National
Information Standards Organization (Z39.48–1984).

10 9 8 7 6 5 4 3 2 1

Copyright Acknowledgments:

The publisher and authors thank those who gave permission to reprint important original
material for the book:

Technomic Publishing Company: Evelyn Ogden and Vito Germinario, *The At-Risk
Student*, pp. 111–118.

Wisconsin Department of Public Instruction. William Berkan, *A Guide to Curriculum
Planning in Suicide Prevention* and *Alcohol and Other Drug Abuse Programs*, various
pages.

We also acknowledge the Montana Office of Public Instruction for making available
several noncopyrighted print sources.

Contents

Preface

Understanding and dealing with death issues with children and youth has always been troublesome for adults. It is one of the most difficult and thoroughly saddening experiences to be faced with the death of a child. If anything, we seem to be more baffled and uncomfortable today with the death of those close to us than we were in earlier times. Direct experience with death has become increasingly remote from everyday life because fewer children die from diseases, the terminally ill die in hospitals rather than at home, and the elderly die in faraway places in retirement centers.

This book is designed to assist schools and communities in achieving better understanding, planning, and management around deaths and high risk situations that involve students and school personnel. Our framework consists of prevention, intervention, and postvention activities, brought together through the schools by planning, training, and coordinating a range of programs with other community agencies, families, and students.

Several unifying elements help bring organization and coherence to the effort. First, we note that accidents, homicides, and suicides are the principal causes of deaths in children and youth and that there is a preventable component in all three. Second, intervention in a possible death and postvention following death provide guidance for designing effective future prevention efforts. Third, prevention approaches involve social skill and self-esteem building, which are important keystones in the broader effort to build resiliency and competency in children and youth.

Although much of the book focuses on understanding and dealing with death, trauma, and grief, it also deals with ways to prevent high risk behavior, violence, and self-destructiveness in a positive, preventive format. *Planning and Managing Death Issues in the Schools* is not viewed as a complete effort by itself. It is part of what can be a total effort by all school and community members to promote life and growth among its children and youth. The book provides a comprehensive guide for developing a complete school plan and conducting it. It also suggests other practical resources for curriculum, counseling, therapy, and collaborative prevention by school and other professionals.

The decision to write *Planning and Managing Death Issues in the Schools* came from a need the authors saw to pull together the best practices that were emerging from a variety of developments related to dealing with suicide and other death issues and preventing violence and self-destructive behavior in children and youth. Experimental efforts in the 1980s to deal with youth suicide and other high risk behaviors and the approaches for developing resiliency in youth through social skill development and positive self-esteem in a set of prevention programs in the 1990s were the main developments. During the same period, students were being assisted to learn to handle grief and loss situations in small groups and postvention activities. Very recently, there is interest in collaboration with school and community services for children, youth, and families. All of these developments, for more than a decade now, suggest combining the best practices into a coherent framework of prevention, intervention, and postvention programs and plans for death issues.

The authors are social work professionals with experience in youth suicide treatment, school staff training, postvention and crisis counseling, and school consultation. They have also designed educational materials for prevention, intervention, and postvention plans and programs in the schools.

Our book is not about death but about life and the quality and struggle of life issues with children and youth. It includes ways to prevent risk and death and accept those things that cannot be fully understood or controlled.

Acknowledgments

The authors acknowledge the assistance of Judy Birch, guidance specialist for Montana State Office of Public Instruction, for her continuing assistance with ideas, criticism, and sources throughout the development of the book.

John Benson, superintendent of the Wisconsin Department of Public Instruction, provided encouragement and resources to the project, including approval for the use of several copyrighted materials developed by the department.

Emily Reinhart carefully did all the copy editing and formatting for the book to make it readable and consistent.

We appreciate the encouragement and good humor of our family members over the two years from the initial idea through the finished copy for the book. Our spouses, Lucy, Ruth, and Idelle were most supportive. All of the children in our three families, Travis, Tricia, Jaclyn, Theresa, Laura, and Bill, inspire us with examples of the wonder, potential, accomplishment, and trauma that young people experience in the world today. Finally, we thank the students, parents, teachers, counselors, and administrators who have shared their knowledge and experiences with us.

Planning and Managing Death Issues in the Schools

1

Introduction

During the past ten years, schools across the country have been systematically dealing with death as it affects those in the school setting. The development began about ten years ago and was combined with the affective curriculum at all grade levels and, in some places, with the drug and alcohol prevention programs directed primarily at the high school level.

Taking action following the death of a student occurred primarily because of national interest in teen suicide, beginning in the 1980s. It was widely publicized in the news and received attention by local communities and schools all over the country. A variety of responses, including counseling services and memorials, were conducted in immediate response to a suicide. Next, short workshops designed to stop teen suicide through providing factual information were conducted for students and in-service training was conducted for teachers. Typically one day or less in length, training sessions contained mortality statistics, how to recognize signs and symptoms of suicide, and what to do if students felt like harming themselves. More recently, there have been prevention efforts through student peer discussion groups and collaboration with related efforts, particularly drug and alcohol prevention programs. Prevention curriculum efforts ranged from elective courses on death and dying at the high school level and brief units in the health curriculum to systematic infusion in the core curriculum at all levels (Wisconsin Department of Public Instruction, 1990).

From the variety of experiences and programs developed in schools and communities in response to child and youth suicide, there has emerged interest in comprehensive, planned efforts to prevent and manage death occurrences in the schools (Patros & Shamoo, 1989; Ogden & Germinario, 1988).

Current approaches represent a new willingness by the schools, in many cases in concert with local communities, to interact with young people directly about a variety of issues, including youth at risk and building resiliency.

In our society, we seem less able now than in previous times to deal with death and other losses. As one writer put it:

In our culture, death and other separations have come to be looked upon as unnatural events, perhaps even sins. In a system that can send people to the moon, why can't we master disease, old age, and the final mystery of death? We're embarrassed, but to pretend we're not, we hide those who remind us, the ill and aged, in segregated facilities, hesitating to answer questions about them. (Bernstein & Gullo, 1977, p. 15)

Since the end of World War II, people of all ages in our society have become further removed from direct experiences with death and, therefore, have less ability to deal with issues related to death and their own mortality. As a result, people are often uncomfortable and lack skills and understanding for expressing shock, grief, sadness, and loss. Grandparents live apart from their children and grandchildren. In their last days, elders are frequently cared for by a third party, usually in a nursing home or other extended care facility. Their passing may not be shared at all with family members. The experience of the death of a grandparent becomes an abstract and distant event.

Until immunizations and public sanitation, it was common for at least one child in the family to die from an epidemic disease before maturity. Older people often lived with their children during their final years, and the family members were around when they passed away. Now, the death of a child from any cause is a rare event, and many would consider it the most extremely stressful event a parent can experience. Little has been done in recent years, however, on a formal or informal basis, to develop ways to cope with such deep personal losses.

Because adults are neither comfortable nor experienced with dealing comfortably with death and loss, they are not adept at helping children deal with those things. The result is an attempt to shield children from having direct experiences or even talking about death, grief, and other losses. In some cases, notably in divorce, the shock and confusion of the child are often ignored by adults, who are preoccupied with their own losses (Wallerstein & Kelly, 1980, p. 36).

It is not uncommon for adults to carry serious lifelong wounds from not being able to deal with trauma and loss which occurred when they were young. "A further complication is that many people who are traumatized at a very early age may not possess the cognitive ability or verbal skills necessary to express their response to trauma at the time: hence, an erroneous or distorted meaning of the event may emerge" (Everstine & Everstine, 1993, p. 103).

Suicide and other forms of tragic death in children are not a new concern. An international psychiatric conference in the 1800s in Europe paid considerable attention to child suicide. *The Sorrow of Young Werther*, by Goethe, a popular novel published in 1774, was considered partly responsible for cluster suicides among youth (Patros and Shamoo, 1989, p. 9).

Prior to the early 1980s, schools and others in local communities did not deal with the reality of suicide in children and youth. In many instances, suicide was underreported and disguised as accidental in coroners' reports. Even in irrefutable suicides, the fact that a young person had taken his or her own life was not discussed in any detail but was treated as a matter that was too humiliating or embarrassing to talk about. Not until the mid-1980s did schools and others begin to realize that significant numbers of children under age 14 did, in fact, commit suicide. States began to report suicide as a major cause of death of young children around 1989 (Montana Department of Health and Environmental Sciences, 1990).

The national movement toward prevention of drug and alcohol use among teens, which began earlier in the 1970s, provided experimentation with methods of reaching youth to prevent and change destructive practices and behaviors. The methods included peer counseling groups, prevention units in the curriculum, special events and assemblies with positive approaches to life events, and self-esteem building activities. Experimentation with a variety of direct educational efforts regarding teen suicide, pregnancy, and drug and alcohol use demonstrated that providing factual information alone would not change or control behavior (Centers for Disease Control and Prevention, 1993, p. 17).

The development of the affective curriculum in the public schools is also a development closely related to increasing students' ability to deal with a variety of death issues. Beginning originally with individual and group activities directed at developing a positive self-image in primary grade children, it broadened to include stress management and personal problem solving (life and social skills) of students. One recent approach by Wexler built upon classroom and peer group approaches with a program of innovative self-management (McWhirter et al., 1993) that provides a self-study approach for adolescents to use to deal with a variety of personal decisions and behaviors.

The Wisconsin State Department of Public Instruction commissioned the development of an extensive suicide prevention curriculum with goals to: provide an experience that promotes self-esteem and positive emotional development for all students; train students, parents, teachers, and other school personnel to identify students at risk; offer a suicide prevention curriculum that is taught to students by or under the supervision of qualified educators; train school psychologists, social workers, counselors, and nurses in crisis intervention and postvention services; develop contingency plans and establish a network within the community to provide support services to students and their families; and encourage students to refer at-risk friends (Wisconsin Department of Public Instruction, 1989, p. 3).

All of the developments of the past 20 years in suicide intervention, affective education, peer counseling, and prevention point to ways to develop comprehensive approaches to prevention and intervention that can be successfully implemented by schools and communities.

The variety of efforts currently available to prevent and intervene in suicide and other deaths provides us with ways to reduce violence and self-destructive behavior in children and youth.

A PICTURE OF DESTRUCTIVE
BEHAVIOR AND CAUSE OF DEATH

Any planning effort should begin with a clear understanding of the nature of the problem. By far, the major cause of death of all young people in every age range is accidents, and it has been so for a long time. Suicide was the second leading cause of death for adolescents but was not mentioned as a significant cause in children under 13–14 years of age for many years. Since around 1990, homicide has become the second major cause of death in young people, and suicide in adolescents has moved to third (*Statistical Abstract of the United States*, 1991, pp. 78, 80, 82).

Some interactive relationships can be inferred about the different causes of death, human developmental theory, and behaviors of children and youth.

There is a pattern of experimentation or self-destructive behavior in many accidental deaths in younger people. Many vehicular accidents and mishaps with firearms are attributed to taking chances in a variety of ways by youth who lack experience and are excited by the opportunity to experiment with the new and dangerous.

Youth risk-taking behavior is combined in many tragic incidents with alcohol and other drugs and with the additional factor of the individual being upset or depressed. In such cases, all these factors can combine in self-destructive ways that cause not only death and permanent injury of the youth who created the incident but also consequences for others who are directly involved.

In a national study of American Indian and Alaskan native youth, a strong correlation was found between suicidal thoughts and other risky behaviors, such as riding in a car without a seat belt or riding with a youthful driver who was under the influence of alcohol or other drugs (Blum et al., 1992). The study corroborated other studies and informal experience about the interrelationships of a variety of health and behavioral risks with injury and death (Centers for Disease Control, 1990).

Clinicians who work with youthful suicide attempters state that the individuals report they did not appreciate the finality and irreversibility of suicidal or other destructive behaviors, even though they knew on an intellectual level about the fatal consequences. Some attempters could visualize family members and friends at their funeral and see themselves dead in a coffin and, yet, report that they assumed that they could come back (Pfeffer, 1986; Peck, Farberow, & Litman, 1985).

However, as we gain more experience from dealing with teen suicide and related tragic death with children and youth, it becomes apparent that young people do, in fact, directly experience incidents of death and extreme violence. Perhaps due to lack of life experience that would give them the perspective and patience to endure through seemingly hopeless or meaningless experiences, they choose to end the pain and pointlessness through suicide. Historically, the adult community has tried to protect children from knowledge about the suffering and death of others. More recently, there has been some interest in helping children and youth become more resilient and develop a variety of means to face all of life's major pressures, including personal despair and suicidal intent (Benard, 1991).

Any comprehensive program designed to prevent suicide must also consider ways to raise self-esteem and personal problem-solving skills and reduce alcohol and other drug use for all youth in the school and community. In dealing with individual cases at risk, it is important to evaluate the personal and family supports as well as the resources and opportunities available to a young person who is suicidal or expresses hopelessness.

Fortunately, prevention programming is in harmony with the multiple causation concepts. This book describes how factors that combine to cause children and youth to engage in self-harm can be alleviated.

SIZING AND NORMALIZING THE PROBLEM

One of the learning tasks of youth, their parents, and those who work with them is to understand the appropriate dimension and importance, or sizing and normalizing the personal concepts of death and suicide.

"Normalizing" refers to using experiential and instructional means to help students see death as something that everybody must deal with. All people everywhere have to come to terms with their own mortality and handle the loss of someone close to them many times in their own lives. How to understand their own feelings and thoughts about a death that profoundly affects them is developmentally important for young people. Understanding is most complete when the student can see the paradox that death is part of the cycle of life.

"Sizing" refers to keeping personal concepts of death in the appropriate perspective or size. If someone trivializes suicide or other death, the idea about it is too small. When someone is overwhelmed or consumed with the notion of suicide or the death of another, they have let a death idea become too big. An important developmental task of older youth is to confront the reality of death and their own life cycle periodically without having to avoid the topic and without becoming either fatalistic or overly fearful about it.

In counseling sessions with suicidal youth in the intervention phase and in teaching units in prevention, the goal is to assist students with making connections about the reality and finality of death as well as achieving expressions about loss and grief. Group and individual grief counseling and debriefing immediately following a death provide the teachable moment to better understand the finality of death as well as appreciate how it is a natural part of the human condition. Hopefully, the combined effort will have the practical result of influencing students to reduce high risk behaviors that harm themselves and others.

WHAT IS THE SCHOOL'S RESPONSIBILITY?

No other entity in the community has a better opportunity or the means to provide prevention, intervention, and postvention activities concerning death issues than the local school system.

Schools are increasingly being called upon to handle a variety of issues and problems that had previously or traditionally been the province of the family, church, or other community institutions. The entry of local schools into these issues, particularly in sex education and moral development, has not occurred without controversy. U.S. public education has long been concerned with the conflict about whether the school should engage in activities beyond basic instruction of students (Lucas, 1972, pp. 526–30). There are those who say that the school has no business outside the traditional core curriculum nor should they be teaching values and behaviors that may be contrary to those of students' families. Other elements in the community strongly advocate the direct involvement of the school in these and other areas of the affective curriculum and preparation for life training and education. One of the authors heard one such parent express the opinion that she expected that student peers of her children should have at least minimal information about sexuality and birth control and that if the schools did not provide it, there was no quality assurance concerning the kind of information all the students received.

However, most current efforts and programs that are being instituted to deal with death can be in harmony with the religious and personal values of students' families and community churches. Probably most people in communities are relieved that something is being done, in contrast to past responses of denial and helplessness.

Rather than the sizeable resistance like that to birth control and sexuality information, there are responses by a few parents who want to deny that their child could be suicidal or seek to shield children from direct confrontations and expressions of grief and sadness concerning the death of someone from school. Such parents are in the minority, and most families would welcome the school's involvement in a holistic, comprehensive approach to death issues that is in harmony with their values.

A unique element of new comprehensive programs to manage death issues through the schools is the development of new understandings of approaches, techniques, knowledge, and some limited research that did not previously exist. We now know some effective and humane things to do that have developed only over the past 10 to 15 years.

There is the caveat that the school must also consider the demands on their resources for launching or expanding their services in this area. It is the authors' experience that not having a plan in place or attempting to ignore a suicide in the school can result in more time being spent trying to respond to uncontrolled crisis and upset. Also, many of the prevention efforts can be integrated into the existing instructional and extracurricular activities. Still, schools must not attempt to do more than is realistically possible, given the resources at their command. Priorities must be set, and the focus must be on what the school can do best and what students need most.

There have been lawsuits brought against local schools in various locations in recent years by parents following the suicide of a child. The assertion brought forward in these proceedings is that the schools should have taken action in cases when they knew or should have known that the student was suicidal. The issue is described in detail in Chapter 3, in which the case is made that the time has passed for the schools to say that the problem is not their concern.

DEVELOPING A COMPREHENSIVE APPROACH

Schools make choices about their approaches and program elements related to death issues based upon current resources, interests, and ability to conceptualize the need and the solutions.

In some localities, the school system and the community will be ready to launch a substantial, comprehensive program, while other places may be inclined to develop a few specific responses.

In the late 1980s, one community received $50,000 from two local philanthropists to immediately develop activities for preventing further teen suicides. Very quickly high schools, youth groups, churches, and service clubs came together to develop crisis services, preventive training for students, and community education. Two other nearby communities of comparable size did very little by comparison. The school district in yet another community took the lead to develop a variety of suicide intervention programs and prevention curriculum without much community financial support.

There is mounting evidence that fragmented youth programs offered from different points of view in the community may not produce results for stopping suicide or related problems. A Carnegie Foundation study on the lack of effectiveness of some local youth programs noted:

Although social indicators clearly point out that young adolescents are making life altering decisions about substance abuse, sexual activity, gang involvement, and a host of other behaviors, some youth organizations cave in to political pressures that they not deal with "controversial" issues or that they not recognize adolescents' autonomy in making behavioral choices. For example, the "Just Say No" programs that seek to prevent substance use and adolescent sexual activity generally provide no practice in active decision making. (Carnegie Corporation of New York, 1992, p. 78)

Often well-intentioned programs have as their principal, but unstated, purpose, to make the adults in the community feel better and to believe that something is being done to prevent dangerous or undesirable behavior. In the experience of the authors, many local youth programs do not even include children and youth in the planning effort. The youthful program participants are brought in during the implementation phase after the adults have made the decisions.

Although in many situations children may not know what is best for them, they certainly know whether the message or the program reaches them clearly and in a manner to which they can meaningfully respond.

In the national campaign to get youth to "Just Say No" to drugs and alcohol in the late 1980s, the bottom of the poster read, "But if you drive, don't drink." Thoughtful young readers caught the contradictory message and doubted if adults believed in the main message themselves or if it was thought that children could be trusted to take it seriously.

THE PREVENTION, INTERVENTION, POSTVENTION FRAMEWORK

Regardless of the specific activities each school chooses to offer, a coherent, integrated plan for approaching and managing death issues in the schools is important. We suggest a unified approach with prevention, intervention, and postvention components.

Prevention

All efforts designed to prevent self-destructive thought and activity, teach ways to deal with grief, reduce violent thought and behavior, promote positive self-worth, and teach skills in personal problem solving as an alternative to violence toward self or others constitute prevention. A planned series of prevention-focused activities enables students to increase their understanding and ability to deal with the concept and reality of death and to cope with ideas about suicide. Children and youth will be able to visualize and plan positive solutions to problems and disappointments as alternatives to violence or despair.

A comprehensive approach involves reviewing all activities of the school for their positive prevention value. Sports, music, science fairs, student government, and other programming can be reviewed for their balance between competition and participation. Positive features of competitive activities are that they help students sharpen abilities, develop self-discipline, and savor the fruits of excellence. Negative values include winning at all costs and feeling devalued for not being chosen for the varsity team or not winning first place when performing adequately or better. Although competition can have positive values, all students also need the experience of enjoying the act of being a participant as well.

Student discipline policies in the school must be evaluated for their effect on self-esteem and self-worth. Care must be taken to focus on the behavior rather than the personality, with emphasis on helping the student to master her/his environment rather than only avoid making a mistake. In Chapter 4, competition, participation, and discipline are described in detail.

A major opportunity for prevention is in the school curriculum. At the K–6 level this can be accomplished largely through changes in the existing core curriculum. Self-esteem building and personal coping strategies should be emphasized in health studies. Selected topics about death, dying, and grieving can be introduced in literature and social studies. Concepts, facts, and techniques for dealing with suicide should not be introduced before sixth grade. *A Guide to Curriculum Planning in Suicide Prevention*, developed by the Wisconsin Department of Public Instruction, provides curricular suggestions by grade level for a prevention curriculum.

At the grade 7–12 level, classic literature and more current, popular works can be discussed to show how youth and young adults have had to grapple with death issues throughout time. Using great literature and history helps students normalize the concept of suicide, loss, grief, and mourning.

Death by violence is a reality for students. They witness the drug-related death of family, peers, and neighbors; the death of relatives and friends through domestic violence, and the random killing of individuals on or near school property during the day.

Very recently the attention of schools and communities has turned toward violence prevention among students. Conflict resolution groups, adult mentoring, and parent education are among the multiple-approach strategies being tried (National Center for Injury Prevention and Control, 1993, pp. 8–12). In addition to reducing violent acts, such programs combined with other positive approaches may help students cognitively seek alternatives to solve problems and get through frustrations.

Prevention efforts of all kinds will not be successful if they are limited to school programs. Changes in the family, local community, and mass media that promote violence all must be a part of the change process. On a national level, in both the public and private sectors, attention must be given to increasing personal economic opportunities for young adults. Much violence among young is related to anger and frustration at not being able to find adequate employment to support themselves or their young families.

Intervention

Efforts to assess, stop, and treat self-harm or destructive behavior that is imminent or in process or to assist survivors in their grief all comprise intervention.

Much of the focus on death issues in the schools has been on youth suicide intervention. The effort differs from other personal and family counseling because of the need for immediate and continuous response to prevent the lethal, irreversible actions of suicidal behavior. Suicide is characterized as the preventable death, and it is true that youth will often choose to live if they can be helped through a suicidal episode.

Training in recognizing signs and symptoms, initial assessment, and referral of suicidal youth must be provided to all school staff who are in contact with students, including (but not limited to) bus drivers, school lunch and custodial personnel, and all professional and administrative staff. School counselors, social workers, and psychologists who engage in direct professional intervention must have specific training in such areas as crisis intervention, specialized counseling, group facilitation, and referral.

The school plan must contain guidelines for responding to suicide attempts. Deciding which staff are designated for immediate intervention, selecting the kinds of ongoing treatment that the school will offer, and developing criteria for referring to outside professionals must be in policy directives. Circumstances under which parents are to be notified must be established, and the range of services that the school will offer must be communicated to the student and the caretaker.

Available peer support group services for students that might have a different focus can be utilized to intervene with suicide attempters as part of the intervention plan.

Efforts must be strengthened by both the schools and community agencies to engage the parents of suicidal youth in actively seeking treatment. As a natural protective defense for the family, parents may try to deny or handle suicidal symptoms by themselves (Everstine & Everstine, 1993, pp. 142–43). Fortunately, the recent attention paid to teen suicide and trauma treatment has provided new tools and possibilities for dealing with the parents and the families of suicidal young people. Subsequent chapters describe options and how to employ them in more detail.

Perhaps the most powerful result of a planned set of intervention measures by the school to deal with the aftermath of death is that it demonstrates true concern for students that they can see. Intervention with suicidal students provides a connection between staff and students who are upset over a friend's suicidal state or their own feelings of helplessness to deal with the changing pressure in their lives. As one of the authors says in training conferences, "We need to say to all of our students that we want them to live." Suicide intervention says to children and youth that they are being monitored and that the school does care deeply that they are alive and want them to stay that way.

Postvention

The responses made by the school immediately following the death of a school member, whether by illness, violence, or suicide, comprise the postvention activities. Decisions about the circumstances, conditions, and responses that the school will employ constitute the postvention plan. Administratively, postvention preplanning is a way to have some control of the situation and to provide needed services that are difficult to mobilize when there is a crisis atmosphere with people who are upset and grieving.

A crisis counseling team is a major component of postvention response that must be fully established in advance. Schools have begun to consider the needs of staff as well as students in offering help to the school community following a death. Questions to be considered in determining the response of the school are: What is the meaning of the particular occurrence to school members? Was it caused by accident, suicide, or illness? Was it expected or unexpected? Was it a single or multiple casualty? Did it occur during the school term or during vacation? What are the wishes of the family and intimate associates? Does the school need the assistance of outside resources in the situation?

Postvention services are important as a humane response to the grief and loss felt by staff and students following the loss of a student, teacher, or other person close to those at the school. It is a way of pausing to be respectful of the life of the one who died and to be concerned for the living in a quiet moment before we rush along with our usual activities.

A fortunate result of effective postvention is that it can have preventive effects. It is a way for students to deepen their understanding of the finality and irreversibility of death and the natural ending of all lives, including their own. The time of reflection that is a part of postvention activity provides a time to evaluate goals and actions, including violence and self-destructive thinking. For some, it will create an atmosphere of receptiveness for other prevention efforts by the school and others in the community.

Finally, the most powerful thing that a school can do is to be good at its regular job. Students and families depend upon the school to be structured and stable, with all its activities directed to the nurturing, growth, and learning of children and youth.

2

Youth at Risk

Recently, high risk and experimental behaviors by children and adolescents have been viewed as having a strong relationship to causes of death and serious injury.

As discussed in the previous chapter, the major causes of death in youth are accidents, homicides, and suicides. There are common factors in the three categories of fatalities. First, they all are high risk behaviors, characterized by seeking thrills through attempting things that most people consider far too dangerous to try. The second factor is the degree of choice and purposeful behavior behind actions associated with high risk situations, including suicide attempts, fast driving, and using guns. Patterns of violence, self-destructiveness, low self-esteem, and lack of life experience to make judgments about the consequences of risk are part of the cause. The third factor is that most of the child and youth deaths and injuries are preventable because they involve choice making and deliberate action on the part of the person who engages in them.

A principal rationale for prevention, intervention, and postvention activities in approaches to death issues with younger people is that a comprehensive approach can reduce accidental death as well as suicides and homicides, through reducing self-destructive behavior, raising self-esteem, and increasing personal problem-solving abilities (Deaton, 1991).

By focusing on the entire spectrum of issues about death that touch young people's lives, it is hoped that students can more fully appreciate life and assume more self-initiated behavior to enrich their own existence.

The narrow focus of concern in the 1970s and 1980s was on teen suicide as the only youth death issue of public concern. More recently, other kinds of death possibilities, particularly accidents and homicides, have engendered concern by schools and communities.

ADOLESCENT DEVELOPMENT

Characteristics of the developmental stages and tasks of youth increase risk factors considerably. Developing into a unique individual with a fully integrated personality is the major task of adolescence (Erikson, 1968). While attempting to mature into adults, youth encounter many blows to their egos, some slight, others major, and many that are self-imposed. Elkind (1975) noted that the desire for approval from others and the deep need to do well causes adolescents to feel that others are watching them all the time, even when they are not.

The sensitivity of youth to opinions about their value as individuals is a point of vulnerability for both suicide and violence toward others. These youth may arrive at thoughts and feelings of hopelessness more quickly than those who are younger or older than they, making them vulnerable to suicide. Youth may perceive criticism and taunts to be more deep and important than they are in reality and severely attack those who put them down.

Adolescents' concept of time is that of the here and now. They have little realization that some important developments take time, which can cause them to become frustrated and develop a sense of futility and impatience when things do not happen instantly. Modern culture encourages a sense of time distortion with its emphasis on fast changing events and instant gratification.

The physical abilities of the brain are faster in youth than in adults, which allows younger people to process information and thoughts very quickly. Unfortunately, they lack life experiences that would help them evaluate occurrences and disappointments. The result is that they make hasty decisions that sometimes have irreversible consequences.

As a result of their characteristic ways of reacting, getting the first low grade is devastating to high school students who have gotten straight "A" grades before. Also, youths who break up with their first real love will feel that love can never happen again and life may as well be over.

AT-RISK BEHAVIOR IN YOUTH

Any behavior initiated by a young person that may have lasting or irreversible negative consequences for them or others involved in the event are considered high risk behaviors. Our focus is on the most serious and irreversible consequences of risk by youth that can result in death or permanent injury. However, youth risk behaviors may be viewed as related, and adolescents sometimes appear to display patterns of behavior that have an increasing level of danger to self or even death. Typical examples of high risk behavior include dangerous driving, suicide attempts, and spontaneous assault.

"At-risk behavior" in children and youth, as it is currently used, has many meanings. It may describe the danger potential for teen pregnancy, drug and alcohol abuse, suicide, violence, dropping out of school, and delinquency. The McWhirters, in their comprehensive book on the subject have defined youth at risk as "a set of presumed cause/effect that place the child or adolescent in danger of negative *future events*" (McWhirter et al., 1993).

At times the adult community becomes greatly concerned about the trouble that young people might get into more than about the actual behavior or occurrence. One of the authors recalls a move in the 1970s to develop prevention programs for "predelinquents." It was soon discovered that it was impossible to prevent or control future delinquent acts in all youth. It also became apparent that "predelinquent" simply described everyone who was not already delinquent and that it was not possible to discriminate between those who would become delinquent and those who would not.

It is our position that the concept of youth at risk should describe concerns that can be clearly stated and predicted as well as deal with issues or behaviors of some importance. Any planned actions directed at prevention or intervention must be carefully matched with specific behaviors and circumstances of risk. Finally, any evaluation of programs must measure the result in reducing the targeted risk, rather than counting activities and participants in organized efforts.

Distinctions can be made between risk behavior potential by older children and adolescents and that of very young children and adults. Generally, a younger child will have less understanding and control over the risk, crisis, or trauma situation. The adults in their lives, including their parents, teachers, and other caretakers, worry and make decisions for them, hoping to protect them from many risks. Coping with risk involves cognitive operations that develop only over time in children and youth (Ryan-Wenger, 1992, p. 256).

Children tend to see risk and threat as being beyond their control and caused by adults or other forces. Later, as adolescents, they begin to assume more personal control and grapple with being in charge of their own destinies.

Adults, by comparison, possess enough knowledge, experience, and judgment to stay out of most dangerous circumstances within their control. If adults engage in risky behavior, it is usually preceded by a conscious evaluation of the relative amount of risk versus the likelihood of a desired outcome. An adult who rescues a child from a burning building decides that the personal danger is less important than the chance to save the life of a child. A sky diver or mountain climber has chosen the value of the thrill of the event over the relative safety of remaining on the ground. Soldiers in combat willingly assume risk from an overriding commitment to their country. Even in planned risks, adults develop and follow safety procedures and use protective clothing and other safety gear to reduce danger.

Youth, on the other hand, have the freedom to get into difficult situations but have not yet fully developed the ability to make appropriate choices. Adolescents have formed the motor skills and are given certain adult privileges not afforded younger children, yet, they lack the life experience to weigh potential risks against the immediate gratifications and benefits of the behavior or situation. Possibly this explains why youth do not change attitudes or their actions toward sexual activity, drinking alcohol, or fast driving as a direct result of factually correct information presented by the adult community.

Teenage driving is a clear example. The newly licensed, 16-year-old driver has had to complete a course, practice under supervision, and pass written and skill demonstration tests to become legally entitled to drive on the streets. His factual information about driving requirements may equal that of adults. His physical attributes of vision, reaction time, and motor skills required to operate a motor vehicle in a variety of situations probably are better than those of most adult drivers. However, his experience is nil compared with adult drivers who have been on the road in a variety of situations for many years. As a result, the youthful driver may react quicker and handle an emergency situation better than an older person, but lacking experience, he may allow himself to get into a difficult situation more easily until he gains a variety of actual experiences in traffic situations.

More recently, planned approaches are being advocated and tried that use counseling, education, and experiential means to enable youth to develop more abilities to evaluate and handle dangerous and harmful situations. These include such things as peer counseling, drug and alcohol education, the affective curriculum, and postvention activities.

CONCERNS OF THE ADULT COMMUNITY

The concern of the adult community for the behavior and safety of its younger members has a long history. Originally, children were viewed as inherently evil and, at the least, mischievous and prone to getting into trouble.

In earlier times, troublesome youth behavior was viewed as a moral issue in which youth were judged as wicked and mischievous by conscious choice or possession by evil spirits. Later, psychological causation was offered that relieved young persons from any individual responsibility for their behavior. More recently, theories and remedies have ranged from counseling and protectiveness by the adult community to punishment and institutionalization.

Some advocate little intervention, noting that delinquent behavior, suicide, and vehicle accidents occur with greater frequency among teenagers and young adults and then diminish rapidly as they get older (Popple & Leighninger, 1993, p. 311). Choosing to do nothing about risky behavior in youth leaves unanswered what to do about those youth who die, harm others, or carry over dysfunctional behavior patterns into adulthood.

At the other extreme are those who take a moralistic approach to child behavior, which serves to blur distinctions among various at-risk behaviors. In this view, if young people can be obedient and compliant to general codes of behavior, there will be no trouble. Sexual behavior, delinquency, drug and alcohol use, and suicidal behavior are often lumped together, even by professional and parent groups, as serious, risky behaviors that are somehow linked in cause and potential harm.

Another tradition is that of parental ownership of the child. Not until the late nineteenth century was the child seen as a person in his or her own right. Prior to that time, children were legally and practically the property of their fathers. The doctrine of *parens patriae* originally meant that the state took over only in the absence of the father by death or desertion. By the early part of the twentieth century, the rights and needs of children as individuals became established (Grossberg, 1993, pp. 113–18).

In modern times, parents invest much in fewer children, and they tend to want even more to protect their children from harm and risk. Indeed, the job of the child and adolescent in the United States is to develop and have experiences that will help make her or him an exceptional human being academically, physically, dermatologically, psychologically, and orthodontically. Extreme investment in children by parents generally focuses on meeting the parents' need to have a perfect child, masked as something for the child's benefit. It puts significant psychological pressure on children and can increase suicide potential, low self-esteem, and fear of failure. It also adds strain to parent-child relationships.

RISK FACTORS HAVE CHANGED OVER TIME

Until the present century, the major childhood risks were life-threatening diseases and becoming orphaned. In colonial America, as many as one-fourth of the children died of epidemic diseases (Wollons, 1993, p. xi).

Currently, the list of serious risks to children is quite different. A small number and proportion of children die from diseases of any sort, and statistically, accidental death, suicide, and homicide have replaced illness as the major causes. The loss of both parents through death has been greatly reduced, but loss of parental presence and support occurs as frequently through family disruption and divorce.

Writing in 1983, Wass noted in her review of research that very little death education was done with children by parents, teachers, or other adults over the previous 20 years. Television, peers, and other unintended random sources in the lives of children provided the main sources of information and concepts. Teachers and parents gave powerful messages by evading and, sometimes, even refusing to share direct information to children and youth about death and dying.

Although not as simple as the "Just Say No" slogan suggests, teaching and encouraging positive self-esteem development, social skills, and personal problem solving hold promise for reducing negative risk.

Improving the opportunity structure for families and reducing child poverty are necessary correlates to high risk in youth. Children from grinding, desperate poverty in inner city schools, lacking even the most basic equipment and supplies, do not readily grasp or relate to positive self-esteem (Kozol, 1991). Any effort that focuses on helping reduce risk factors must include a frank appraisal of chances for success in the environment in which the child operates. At the very least, it must include ways to help the child correctly assess what it takes to be competitive in an environment of few opportunities and many seekers. At best there could be a combined approach by the community to make more opportunities available to children and young adults while assisting them to become more sturdy, prepared individuals able to face adversities.

RISK SITUATIONS IN DEATH
ISSUES MANAGEMENT

Any effort to reduce actual preventable deaths in young people is the highest priority goal. The numbers of lives lost in the top categories of causes of death in children and youth is unacceptable when compared with other fatality numbers in other situations about which society is greatly concerned.

Accidental deaths claim more children and youth than any other single cause. Partly this is due to their being less likely to die from congenital conditions, which take infants and toddlers, or the vascular and malignant diseases that claim middle-aged and older adults. However, a large portion of accidental deaths of younger people are related to risk taking or disregarding standard precautions. A 1991 nationwide study of students in grades 9–12 by the National Centers for Disease Control reported that only about 28 percent of them wore seatbelts in motor vehicles all the time. Respondents used motorcycle helmets 39 percent and bicycle helmets only 1 percent of the time. There was little difference between male and female students (*Journal of School Health*, 1991, pp. 439–43).

Teen suicide deaths between the ages of 15 and 19 are variously estimated as being between 4,800 and 6,500 per year and correspond with the highest annual fatality rates of U.S. soldiers in the Vietnam War. It is also about the same as the average number of deaths from structure fires across the country (Deaton, 1991, p. 1).

The number of children and youth killed by guns has received recent national attention. Of the more than 5,300 youth aged 15–19 killed by firearms in 1991, only 11 percent were accidental shootings. The president of the National Association of Children's Hospitals noted that polio was claiming 3,152 adults and children in 1952 and the nation considered it a national epidemic requiring the highest efforts to eradicate (*Missoulian*, 1993, p. c-4).

Self-destructive behavior and violence also spill over into other situations beyond those with fatal implications. Permanent injury to self and others is an immediate consequence. Drive-by shootings that claim innocent victims are vivid examples. Less obvious are those situations where a friend was injured in an auto accident with a young driver who was going too fast.

The predisposition to cause self harm or violence may develop during childhood or adolescence but not be carried out until much later. Suicide that is not completed until young adulthood reflects self-destructive patterns learned earlier. Spousal violence tragically demonstrates a way of reacting to frustration that was learned in the family and not discouraged through the school or community.

Serious violence toward others, such as shootings in the workplace or schools, reflects long-term predisposition to eliminate the source of frustration by eradicating it. Impulsive violence toward others without using self-restraint or trying alternative peaceful ways is reinforced with images in the media that show the hero doing away with those who are seen as problems. Violence as a solution is regularly presented even in children's cartoons on Saturday morning television. It could be argued that children could distinguish between the fantasy shown on television and films and real life situations where violence did not happen. Increasingly, however, real life in the homes and neighborhoods of young people approximates the shootings, knifings, beatings, and robberies depicted in the media.

Of no less concern is self-defeating and destructive behavior that is developed in youth and carried over into essential life tasks, such as school and job performance and marital and family responsibilities.

BUILDING SELF-ESTEEM AND SKILL MASTERY
TO REDUCE HIGH RISK BEHAVIOR

Beginning with building positive self-esteem, children need to develop mastery in a variety of social and technical skills. Their good feelings about themselves do not come only from others telling them that they are people of worth; they also must learn to be successful in their world and gain self-esteem from being productive. Earlier attempts to develop self-esteem in students only by teaching them their personal rights and reinforcing feeling good about themselves through group and individual activities in classroom settings did not produce lasting results (Weir, 1991, pp. 11–20). Self-esteem becomes embedded through competence at a variety of life tasks and situations. In addition to the classroom, it is also reinforced in other school situations and home and community interactions.

Certainly one part of helping children and youth become competent, able adults is assisting them to understand and personally manage death situations that affect them. By directly and quickly responding after a death has occurred, adults demonstrate mastery of loss, grief, and mourning, so that a death does not become just a situation over which young people have no control.

Speaking directly and factually about the fatality reinforces for older children and youth that death is irreversible and final and that every alternative must be used to prevent untimely death for self and for others. Prevention approaches through the curriculum can teach children that death is a natural happening in the lives of people and that everyone must learn ways to enhance their own safety, be careful of the lives of others, and grapple with the loss of friends and relatives.

Intervening in potential suicides and violence at the school shows students that it is possible to stop preventable deaths and other harmful events. It is not necessary to stand by and witness violence to self or others without taking appropriate direct action or summoning help when the situation is beyond the resources of the student to control.

It is not possible to help young people master life without also assisting them to understand and deal with death. Put more simply, those who deal well with death can also be those who deal well with life.

APPROPRIATE RESPONSES OF SCHOOL AND COMMUNITY TO RISK

The adult community must begin with a clear understanding of truly risky behavior of children and youth that requires a response as opposed to experimental, nonrisky behavior of less concern. Some efforts to change the choices or actions of youth reflect an overprotective posture of a group of adults.

In a training conference presentation, one of the authors was describing the distinction between risky behavior and relatively safe experimental actions by high school students. To illustrate, he said that he wanted his own children occasionally to try a drink containing alcohol. After the presentation, a local parent who was a leader in a teen alcohol and drug prevention program told him most emphatically that if no children ever took the first drink in their lives that none could ever become addicted. The entire focus of her efforts was on a total abstinence program for students rather than on choice, moderation, and self-control, which would be more appropriate and have a greater chance of success, in the author's view.

Following a detailed assessment and inventory of risk problems, attention is directed to efforts that are matched to the problem and have a strong likelihood of success. Jack Frymier, in his study of children at risk (1992, p. 53), notes that professionals as well as parents tend to look for solutions based on their preconceived idealogies rather than on the facts. A total abstinence campaign against alcohol use or premarital sex directed to high school students is attractive to school personnel and parents as a way to comfort themselves with the belief that if children can be totally shielded from the identified practice, there will never be a problem to worry about. However, abstinence and factual information programs have been shown to have little effect on the attitudes and actions of youth who are engaging in the negative behavior, although the effort may provide positive reinforcement for those youth who do not tend to engage in the undesired practice.

An understanding of what is occurring, who is doing it, and what people are getting out of the risky behavior is necessary before strategies are selected to deal with it. Otherwise, there is the likelihood that professionals will select strategies that are sensible to them rather than matched with what is needed.

The Task Force on Teen Suicide in the U.S. Department of Health and Human Services in the late 1980s found that the most frequently recommended programs to stop teen suicide were

developing affective education programs to promote positive self-esteem and exploring positive alternatives to negative behavior,

implementing early diagnosis and treatment of suicide attempts,

expanding school-based screening programs to catch suicidal and related behaviors,

developing crisis centers and suicide hot lines,

training mental health professionals in the community to recognize and treat youth who attempted suicide and had related conditions, and

restricting access to lethal means of committing suicide or inflicting violence on others. (Berman & Jobes, 1991, p. 32)

In commenting on the six frequently used approaches to reduce youth suicide, Berman and Jobes noted that there have been no long-term studies to determine if any of the programs have had a measurable effect on reducing the incidence of suicide or increasing positive behavior or attitudes (1991, p. 36).

Experts who have made detailed recommendations for designing effective programs to reduce risky behavior and develop resilient, confident, productive young citizens all recommend concerted action by the community, school, and family (Benard, 1991; Melaville & Blank, 1993).

Each recognized that where efforts exist, they are piecemeal and not usually coordinated with each other. Frymier (1992, p. 53) observes that school personnel tend to think about what they can do that might help rather than carefully studying the problem to see what solution might work, for example, developing a workshop or teaching unit for students on building self-esteem when the problem is lack of income, jobs, or housing.

The programs of many community youth organizations are developed by adults, and some have national agendas with little local relevance, according to findings of the Task Force on Youth Development and Community Programs funded by the Carnegie Corporation (Carnegie Corporation of New York, 1992, p. 78). The report went on to say that controversial topics such as sexuality often were avoided, or when they were approached, didactic presentations were made that did not provide ways to practice the behavior or skills required.

Community children and youth programs also tend to look at numbers of participants and at starting programs in new communities without regard for the benefit to youth and family needs in local areas.

The public has looked at street gangs in a totally negative light because the focus of their activities has been dangerous to the community, but the processes and needs fulfilled by the gangs have been very functional. There is a strong sense of belonging and group purpose that the youthful members have had a share in shaping. Language, clothing, and other symbols are relevant to the neighborhood where the members live. Activities are appropriate to the economic and social conditions of the youths who belong. Most street gangs were not developed by their members as a response against adults or the local community but are the result of a lack of positive, relevant activities.

Many families, and parents more particularly, are not as available to their children as is needed for proper nurturing. Some adults in two-parent families and most single parents are occupied full time at work or school. The U.S. system for child rearing has traditionally assumed that the mother would be home while the father worked as family breadwinner. When that practice started to change in the late 1960s with many mothers going to work full time, nothing was added elsewhere to see to the needs of children. Much of the volunteer work done by parents at the school and in community groups provided a natural link between the child and the community, and a great portion of that natural system has been lost.

GOALS FOR PROGRAMS TO ASSIST YOUTH AT RISK

Concerted efforts to reduce risky actions and lethal situations must begin with a careful assessment of conditions rather than the implementation of a preconceived program by the adult community. Programs that are implemented after careful planning must contain activities that allow children and youth to participate in their design and must contain ways to practice the desired behavior.

Community, school, family, and students must all act together to ensure the development of coordinated efforts that promote safety and surround children with a reasonable, nurturing environment. Success can be further assured if the adults in the community also attempt to be good examples by modeling the thinking and actions that promote safe behaviors that are respectful of self and others.

3

Developing a School Plan

Traditionally, U.S. schools have had a unique role in society that has been expanded by the social changes of the past 50 years. As described in the two preceding chapters, students today live in a world of drugs, teen pregnancy, violence, family disruption, suicide, and doubt over their economic future. These are not historically unique stressors, but the extent to which they exist today reflects the steadily declining positive influence of adults on youth (Miller et al., 1992). The community has not developed a clear position on the school's role in death issues, in part because there has not been sufficient knowledge until recently. Solutions will differ for each school district and community and will reflect the combination of responsibilities each is willing to adopt.

Educational programs must be able to answer the following questions: How will the content benefit the students and better prepare them for independence? How will material support the parents in their child-rearing task? How will the information be presented in an educationally competent manner? These broad questions become complicated when applied to suicide prevention and other death issues. The purpose of this chapter is to provide a framework for developing a school suicide prevention and death issues program and describing its major components.

The business of education is education, but the definition of education varies from community to community. Most citizens share the common expectation that students should graduate from the public school system prepared to either seek further education and training or to be self-supporting. Emphasis on the basics of reading, writing, and arithmetic is not enough to insure that the facts and basic skills taught in the school will be applied to the student's life after high school. The decision about additional material and skills to be taught often creates educational controversy. It is useful to consider the generally accepted responsibilities that schools have toward students and families to decide what should be offered in a total curriculum that includes developmental as well as instructional needs of the student.

1. Schools are responsible for establishing a basic curriculum that provides students with the opportunity to learn the necessary academic and functional skills to live in society.
2. Schools are responsible for identifying and assisting students who are having difficulty with the curriculum to overcome learning problems and to achieve appropriate educational goals.
3. Schools are responsible for insuring the health and safety of all students while they participate in classroom or extracurricular activities.
4. Schools are responsible for supporting family functioning by giving parents additional insight into the needs of their children.
5. Schools are responsible for involving families in the educational lives of their children.

These five responsibilities are a summary of the general goals of school programming. They must be carefully considered when designing suicide and other sudden death crisis intervention and prevention programs that the schools implement. Considering these responsibilities will avoid alienating parents or destroying the opportunity to help students in crisis (Fullan & Stiegelbauer, 1991).

SCHOOL LIABILITY ISSUES

Although the responsibility of schools is becoming clear in a general sense, the relationship between specific programming and the details of legal responsibility is still emerging and being tested. Legal responsibility is based on two factors: the directives in statutes and the school responsibility based on what a reasonable and prudent individual would do in a given circumstance (Robertson, 1988). In the case of the professional educator, that which is reasonable and prudent will also be defined by how good practice in education is defined. Good practice will demand that educators keep students from harm to the extent possible. As the adults who are responsible for children during the school day, educators must exercise whatever action is necessary to assure the health and safety of the students in their care (Simon, 1988).

Laws do not impose an absolute responsibility on educators for the prevention of youth suicide or for providing a curricular approach to other death issues. However, in those states where the legislature has assigned the responsibility of addressing the prevention of youth suicide to schools, the law also implies an expectation that schools will meet prevailing educational standards and practices in suicide prevention, including the safety and health of students in their care.

Laws, such as those in Wisconsin, define what material is taught to students and what information professional staff should know regarding suicide. Wisconsin requires that students be taught:

The skills needed to make sound decisions, knowledge of the conditions . . . and the signs of suicidal tendencies, knowledge of the relationship between youth suicide and the use of alcohol and controlled substances . . . and the knowledge of the available community services. Instruction shall be designed to help prevent suicides by pupils by promoting the positive emotional development of pupils. (Wisconsin Statutes, 1985, s15.377(7), s115.365, s118.01(2)(d)7)

The same law also requires that professional staff of public and private schools and county departments of social services, mental health, and developmental disabilities all be given training in the same areas as students. The purpose of the law is to "enable and encourage public and private schools to develop programs which will prevent suicide among minors" and to instruct professional staff in the "proper action to take when there is reason to believe that a minor has suicidal tendencies" (*Wisconsin Statutes*, 1985, 15.365).

Many schools are reluctant to teach students about suicide or other death issues for fear that they will encourage students to attempt suicide or other high risk behaviors. They also question the addition of another subject to an already crowded educational program. Further, they argue that teachers are not prepared to present what is essentially mental health material to students, especially when such information is as sensitive as suicide and other death issues. Within the context of legal liability, these arguments would have potentially little weight in a court where the state law is clear that schools have a responsibility to teach specific material regarding suicide. Research in suicide prevention and positions taken by the American Association of Suicidology have demonstrated that talking about suicide does not cause an individual to attempt suicide (Pfeffer, 1989). Wisconsin law does not require that an entire course on suicide prevention be taught, only that the listed topics be included in the curriculum. Further, it does not dictate how topics are to be taught, and it leaves instructional decisions up to educators (*Wisconsin Statutes*, 1985).

Finally, school staff have a duty to warn parents if the children are endangering themselves or others or becoming endangered by others (Tarasoff, 1976). The duty to warn applies to the possibility that a student is contemplating suicide or engaging in other life-threatening behavior. If the staff have reason to believe that a student is thinking of suicide, they are obligated to inform the parents and to notify the appropriate mental health facility for an assessment of the student's risk of suicide.

Schools are not expected to be able to prevent all suicides, nor are they expected to recognize every instance of potential suicide or violence. Schools are expected to make a good faith effort to protect students by informing their staff of what to look for and what to do when they are suspicious of a student's potential for self-destruction.

However, schools may incur liability if they act in such a manner as to cause a student to attempt suicide or otherwise harm themselves. Although no school or educational professional would intentionally set out to cause a student to attempt suicide, they might be guilty of negligence in their actions toward a student, which could lead to the opportunity and means for the student to act on their suicidal intent. If, for example, a student who was known or suspected of being suicidal were to be left unsupervised and would subsequently attempt to take his or her own life, the school and the educator involved could be considered liable. On the other hand, liability might not be an issue if the school staff person did not have information that a suicidal danger was present (Bongar, 1991).

Schools who wish to protect their students from suicidal behavior and also protect themselves from legal liability need to provide whatever services the state legislature defines as the minimum, establish a written plan that outlines the suicide prevention plan (including prevention, intervention, and postvention), inform parents of the existence of the plan, inform parents whenever their child is thought to be suicidal, provide on-site assessment of the suicidal risk presented by a student or group of students to determine the need for referral, and conduct an evaluation of the effectiveness of the plan on a regular basis.

THE LIMITS AND SCOPE OF THE SCHOOL'S RESPONSIBILITY

The school's responsibility to develop a plan for prevention of suicide and other crises is based on two factors. First, although schools are not child-care institutions, their responsibility to insure the health and safety of the students during the school day implies a proactive stance for anticipating and intervening in high risk behaviors of students. Second, the professional goals and the personal involvement of educators with students require a concern for the emotional, as well as the educational, development of the students in their charge. The two factors are based on both legal and professional responsibilities as well as the positive character of educators. However, individual educators may react to death issues with denial or avoidance if they do not have a clear understanding of the issues, the district crisis intervention policy and procedures, access to an institutional support system, and training to implement guidelines and practices.

District policy dealing with students in crisis is designed to help those who need immediate assistance and to insure that educators will have a directed course of action to take during a crisis situation. The level and type of response established by the district provides an institutionalized control that assists teachers with their emotional response to the situation and that provides them with a constructive way to show their concern for individual students. Schools must be aware of legal constraints and requirements, community reactions, students' needs, accepted postvention concepts, and staff limitations when establishing a suicide prevention and death issues crisis plan.

An effective school plan must address both the legal responsibility of the district and the emotional needs of staff and students. It must contain elements of prevention, intervention, and postvention. Each of these elements needs to be further broken down into parts that address the staff, the students, and the community.

WHEN SHOULD A PLAN BE DEVELOPED?

Historically, the development of a suicide prevention plan has begun only after the community and/or the school district has experienced a suicide or a series of nearly fatal suicide attempts. As a result, most plans are limited to intervention, do not contain prevention plans, and may be hastily formed without all components. Later, because suicides and other crises do not normally occur predictably over a given period, the plan is forgotten. By contrast, a well-planned approach is begun before an emergency exists. It includes school and community agencies in its development and deals not only with suicide and sudden death issues but also with serious youth risk behaviors. In a comprehensive approach, it is possible to use the professional literature and outside experts in various specialties to design a plan that will work for the community. It allows all parties to examine the resources available, establish protocols for their use, and establish a working relationship among agencies and individuals.

WHAT ARE THE FUNDAMENTAL PRINCIPLES OF A PREVENTION PLAN?

Principle One: The Plan Should Be Community Based/School Focused

Schools are not prepared, nor do they have the mandate, to implement a comprehensive and effective prevention plan alone. They do have an important contribution to make, and they represent the single location in the community where children are required to spend a substantial portion of the day. Prevention requires that adults who have access to children understand the specific needs of each age group, are trained to see the warning signs of impending difficulties in individuals and groups of children, are prepared and comfortable with taking initial action to avoid harm to youth, and have the trust of young people.

Community agencies, on the other hand, have access to the resources needed to provide support and treatment to children and families who are in distress. The recognition by the school and the community agency that they are both essential to the implementation of the plan is critical to its success.

Principle Two: Adult Preparation and Training Must Be Done Prior to Offering Services

If students are told that a community or a district has instituted a prevention and crisis response plan, they can reasonably expect to receive help in crisis situations from the outset. Schools and other cooperating community agencies are obligated to have appropriate staff and other resources in place from the time services are first implemented.

Principle Three: The Plan Should Be
Based on a Youth Risk Behavior Approach

Although suicide is the most frequent focus of the prevention plan, it is not a single, isolated reaction by a student and should be seen as only one part of the effort. It is the culmination of a series of events with which the student has not been able to cope. As students experience repeated failure to resolve problems, they can develop the hopeless emotional state that characterizes suicidal crisis. Negative problem-solving behaviors may include acting out, using alcohol and other drugs, violence, running away, and self-destructive acts. It is imperative that student behavior be understood as a continuum that can lead to several outcomes. Prevention, therefore, has as its primary focus the encouragement of more effective problem-solving behaviors through the strengthening and support of individual students. Any activity that is aimed at reducing the effects of teen pregnancy; violence; dropping out of school; alcohol and drug use, abuse and neglect; and isolation also has a positive effect on preventing suicide (Pfeffer, 1989).

Principle Four: Information about Suicide and
Other Youth Risk Behaviors Should Be
Given in Small Group Presentations

In prevention programs, small groups allow students to interact with a trusted adult in a setting where suicide is only one topic discussed. It reduces the anxiety often felt by individuals toward death topics, allows individual class members to support one another, and encourages discussion. The small size of the group allows the adult to provide individual attention and assistance to class members who are upset by the presentation or who have highly personal questions. Small groups and individual counseling are essential after a completed suicide or other death to allow adults to assess the effect of the death on survivors and to assist students in dealing with shock and loss as they work through their grief experience. Crisis response services to students individually and in small groups are important to identify those who need follow-up with local mental health services.

Principle Five: Suicide Prevention Material Should Be
Integrated into the Existing School Curriculum

Single event presentations should be avoided unless associated with regular curricular goals and with time for students to immediately process the material. Much of the existing curricula are well suited to the inclusion of suicide prevention materials and discussions about other death issues. For example, an English course might include in the study of Romeo and Juliet a discussion of the signs that indicated that suicide was a possibility and require the students to rewrite the ending of the play to show how the suicides could have been prevented. Similar adaptations can be made in high school psychology, social studies, or home economics classes.

Integration of suicide prevention and death issues material is best understood if it is considered as a part of the youth risk approach. Kindergarten students who learn to respect themselves and others, who learn to trust adults, and who learn how to ask for help are beginning the process of either avoiding the problems of later years or learning how to deal with them more appropriately. As students become more developmentally ready to understand the concepts, suicide may be addressed directly (Pfeffer, 1986). Middle school pupils are ready to deal with the concepts of depression and the need to get help for problems they cannot handle themselves (Konopka, 1973; Hill, 1980). They are at a prime age to develop healthy relationships with the adults around them, including school staff. High school students are prepared to address ways to recognize the signs of suicide in their peers. They are also ready to take the responsibility of reporting the need for help to an adult regardless of a friend's request to keep it secret. The *Wisconsin Guide to Curriculum Planning in Suicide Prevention* (Berkan, 1990) details plans from kindergarten through high school.

Principle Six: Involve Students in Suicide and Other High Risk Behaviors Prevention Plans, Especially in the Intervention Phase

Intervention may be considered secondary prevention in that it is geared toward recognizing and intervening before an individual attempts self-destructive behavior. The chances of a student telling another student that they are suicidal or planning to engage in other high risk behavior are greater than those of the student telling an adult. Most existing prevention plans include teaching students to recognize the signs of high risk behavior in other students and encouraging them to seek help from an adult. Students may also assist the school in raising the awareness of the general student body to the need to help each other when in crisis and in legitimizing the imperative to never keep a secret in suicidal or other high risk situations (Curran, 1987; Lawrence & Ureda 1990).

Principle Seven: Suicide Prevention Plans Should Include Recognition of the Social, Emotional, and Medical Aspects of the Problem

The majority of the actions that are taken as youth suicide prevention stem from observable phenomena that adults or peers recognize as denoting suicidal potential (Davidson & Linnoila, 1991). The current focus on recognizing observable signs of suicide such as withdrawal, unusual weight gain or loss, verbal expressions, and giving away prized possessions often can serve to obscure a complete consideration of the multiple causes of suicidal behavior. Proponents of medical and psychosocial theories of causation often ignore the probability that suicide, like other human behavior, has multiple causes. Those individuals responsible for developing and implementing suicide prevention and crisis intervention plans must avoid accepting one view while rejecting the other. In dealing with the treatment of suicidal individuals, consideration of a medical reason for their behavior is important. Research has established that the amount of serotonin present in an individual's body is related to suicide (Pfeffer, 1986, p. 76).

Principle Eight: Prevention Plans Include Expanded Activities and Opportunities for Students

Adult mentors, part-time employment, recreation, and community service opportunities for students are examples of meaningful activities and interactions in the community. In today's society, because of poverty or lack of adult support, some students are faced with the need to be independent and care for themselves before they have developed the necessary skills.

The importance of adult mentors to young people as they move away from their families and increasingly make independent decisions lies in the need of youth for an adult who will listen to what is happening in their lives.

Employment allows young people to learn more than good work habits. Possibly its greatest lesson is that by investing time and effort, individuals are able to gain control over other aspects of their lives. The money earned can be used to purchase something that fulfills a need and gives the youth independence from parent controlled funds. It is important that employment of students be limited to 10–15 hours weekly to avoid interfering with the other important developmental areas of the student's life, such as educational and social experiences.

Recreation is important because it renews the emotional energy of the individual, provides youth with experience in planning group activities, and gives youth the opportunity to observe potential adult mentors who are acting as advisors to the program. Organized groups, such as sports teams, drama clubs, chorus, or a debate team, provide students with an identity during the time they are developing a unique identity. Community service is an opportunity to develop self-esteem through helping others. Adults who help organize such activities need to help young participants understand the importance of their contribution to others and to society.

Finally, a comprehensive prevention plan will also include intervention activities that will have as their primary goal stopping students from harming themselves and others. Those responsible for initiating plans must use well-proven information available now and intervene in a timely way.

DEVELOPING THE PLAN

Initial planning of an effective suicide prevention and death issues approach or the revision of an existing plan starts when one or two individuals identify the need to do so. A steering committee of administrators, line staff, community professionals, parents, and students is assembled. The members must share a desire to carefully assess needs of young people and be willing to contribute resources such as time, ideas, staff, and funds to the effort.

Collaboration requires partners to put aside individual agendas in favor of common goals. They need to share leadership, pool resources, and accept public responsibility for what the collaborative does or does not accomplish. This means putting aside organizational and personal differences and making long term commitments. (Melaville et al., 1993)

The planning process can be divided into eight phases, each important to the overall success of the prevention program:

1. Defining the problem
2. Identifying the available resources
3. Selecting a response model

4. Building support
5. Designing the community based/school focused plan
6. Gaining approval of the plan
7. Implementing
8. Evaluating

Defining the Problem

Planners need to keep in mind the interrelated nature of causation in the negative behaviors of youth. It must be clearly understood that the plan will be one that integrates the prevention and intervention efforts of other youth programs with the approaches for preventing suicide and other high risk behaviors. Data are available in most communities that will allow the group to prepare a locally relevant report on the condition of children and youth in the community. Most states maintain information on the number of children who are involved in drug and alcohol abuse, are abused or neglected, live in poverty, come from single-parent families, drop out of school, are involved in violence, are pregnant, or may be experiencing similar pressures. The economic data and trends in the community and information about the local students' experience with these problems can be added to illustrate the impact on the community (Figure 3-1). It is particularly important to obtain the opinions of community professionals and local leaders in this regard. The information should incorporate not only descriptive but also interpretive statements. Combining a description of the findings with the group's interpretation of the information allows for an objective and reasonably comprehensive view of unique needs of youth in the community to reduce the tendency to develop programs for youth based on preconceived assumptions.

FIGURE 3-1
General Community Data Sheet

1. INCOME
   Range: High _____ Low _____ Average _____
   Percent below Poverty Level _____

2. POPULATION _____
   Increase/Decrease Past 5 Years _____

3. LAW ENFORCEMENT DATA
   Felony Arrests _____   Convictions _____
   Misdemeanor Arrests _____   Convictions _____
   Juvenile Arrests/Convictions
       Robbery   _____ / _____
       Drugs   _____ / _____
       Alcohol   _____ / _____
       Speeding   _____ / _____
       Weapons   _____ / _____
       Vandalism   _____ / _____

4. SOCIAL SERVICES DATA
   AFDC Caseload _____ Increase/Decrease Past 5 Years _____
   Number of Children on AFDC _____
   Abuse Reports _____ Increase _____ Decrease _____
       Substantiated _____ Unsubstantiated _____
   Neglect Reports _____ Increase _____ Decrease _____
       Substantiated _____ Unsubstantiated _____

5. EDUCATIONAL DATA
   Percent of Adults with College Degree _____
   Percent of Adults with High School Diploma _____
   Percent of Adults with GED/Other Training _____

   Number of School Age Children _____
       Grades Kindergarten–5   _____
       Grades 6–8   _____
       Grades 9–12   _____
   Dropout Rate Past 5 Years _____
       Present Year   _____
       Year 2   _____
       Year 3   _____
       Year 4   _____
       Year 5   _____

CHILD HEALTH INFORMATION
Percent of Children Vaccinated   _____
Confirmed Pregnancy under Age 18 _____
Emergency Room Admissions   _____
   Auto Accidents   _____
   Family Violence   _____
   Gunshot Wounds   _____
   Confirmed Suicides   _____
     Attempts   _____
     Completions   _____

Identifying Community Resources

The effort should include clear statements of the interests of community agencies and contributions they can make in becoming involved with the prevention plan. The following agencies and groups comprise a minimal list of potential resources.

Schools

Schools have special programs and staff that can be utilized in establishing a youth risk prevention approach serving students and their families, including curricular resources. After family, the school is the center of the young person's life. All school age children are required by law to attend school, and some mechanism exists to insure attendance in most, if not all, states. Long-term relationships develop between students and teachers and provide a rich point of contact for services to youth in difficulty. The professional and personal commitment of educators to children prepares them to participate in prevention programming that is directed and designed to be implemented in the school setting.

Public Human Service Agencies

Included in public human service agencies are those services needed to make a coordinated, collaborative prevention effort. They include social services, child protection, mental health, and public health nursing. In Wisconsin, the law that mandates social services clearly states that the purpose of social service departments is to use the public resources to provide for the welfare of state citizens (*Wisconsin Statutes*, Chap. 46). Similar wording exists in most states and allows agencies to explore developing direct social service projects for families.

Private Social Service Agencies

Catholic Social Services, Lutheran Social Services, Family Services, and Children's Service Society are examples of private agencies that may have staff, experience, and funds to assist in the effort. Historically, private agencies have developed programs to fill gaps in public services and have pioneered work for developing new services, which makes them a natural ally in designing new and innovative approaches to prevention. An example of the willingness to be innovative is the Families and Schools Together program developed by Llyn McDonald, Dane County (Wisconsin) Family Services Association (personal interview). In the program, families join with the Family Services Associaiton and the local school to work on parenting skills, social and emotional development, and educational improvement. The ability of educators and parents to collaborate for the benefit of children is the major focus of the program. Dramatic academic, social, and parenting skill gains have resulted in families that many professionals felt did not have the potential for growth.

Youth Agencies

The YMCA, YWCA, Boy Scouts, Girl Scouts, and 4-H Clubs are all potential resources to be included in school and community collaboration. A major value of youth organizations in preventing destructive behavior is the opportunity they provide for positive youth/adult interaction. Youth are given the opportunity to seek out adult mentors to assist them in resolving problems and developing a larger selection of successful problem-solving behaviors. The experience supplements and enhances parent/child relationships by allowing young persons to test reactions of adults other than their parents to various problem-solving behaviors.

Business and Local Civic Organizations

Increasingly, the positive influence of businesses and civic clubs has been felt in service-oriented community programs. Aid Association for Lutherans, Knights of Columbus, Blue Cross/Blue Shield, and other mutual insurance groups have donated time and money to youth projects. Service clubs such as Kiwanis and Exchange have youth services as national program initiatives.

Individual small businesses have enthusiastically given time and money to local efforts. Some individual businesses are youth oriented and provide recreational opportunities to students and profit to the owners, and they can play important roles in prevention programs.

One midwestern funeral director became concerned over the number of young people who were dying in alcohol related or suicidal incidents and approached the local school district to offer assistance. During his meetings with the district, several needs emerged. Budgetary limitations had prevented the school from devoting staff time to suicide prevention programs and from purchasing audio-visual materials for instructing students. The funeral director agreed to research suicide through his professional organization, prepare himself and any staff members from the school to present the information to the students, and purchase the audio-visual materials for the school. As a result of his added assistance, the district designed a sound suicide prevention curriculum and was motivated to review and update their suicide and sudden death crisis plan.

Churches

Most churches have youth groups that provide recreational opportunities and guidance to students, and they have established a record of credibility with youth. They also have knowledge, funds, and other resources they may contribute. Additionally, they provide another entree into the family that can be used to sensitize parents to recognize any special needs of their children and educate them about available resources. Church groups are also a fertile area to recruit adult mentors and other volunteers to enhance the overall implementation of the plan. Church sponsored activities and educational programs for members provide opportunities to contact people who may not readily seek out schools and community agencies for assistance with youth and family problems. Finally, when dealing with death issues, the emotional support and other assistance given by the church to survivors is an integral part of assisting children and youth to understand grief and loss.

Parents and Community Volunteers

Every community has its share of adults who are involved in activities with children and youth for a variety of reasons. Some may have children or grandchildren of their own, which motivates them to become involved in various groups; others may enjoy the company of young people with whom they do not have a direct connection; and still others may recognize that the community's children need support and guidance in order to insure its future. Whatever the positive motivation, community adults are resources that are needed in the overall plan to insure success. They can be direct contact workers with children and youth, or they can be spokesman for community programs to obtain popular and political support for what needs to be done.

One of the authors is well acquainted with a project in Stoughton, Wisconsin, where the school and the public social service department enlisted assistance from individuals to obtain funds and change local ordinances that would provide for the renovation and remodeling of an existing building for a youth center. Some of the volunteer adults solicited donations from individuals and businesses in the community, others lobbied the city council for authorization for the project, and still others obtained the support of service groups. The result was a facility for students in the community that was a natural meeting place for adults and young people. Programming decisions are made by youth with the advice and assistance of adults, resulting in a supportive environment for students. In such an environment, young people feel free to seek out adult advice and involvement in several areas of their lives. The result would not have been possible without the network of individual adults who supported its development in a variety of community arenas. The center has become a focal point in the prevention of alcohol and drug abuse, suicide, violence, and other negative youth behaviors.

In order to locate resources and measure their value for the plan, it is necessary to conduct an assessment. Potential resources should initially be nominated by those individuals who have been recruited to participate in the planning process. It is critical that elected officials be invited to participate in the planning phase. They should formulate a statement of purpose, which can be included with the survey, and develop a series of questions about the interest, willingness, and actual resources the subject of the survey can bring to the larger group.

As opinion leaders who are familiar with a wide range of needs and services, they could be asked questions such as: What are the major problems which our children and youth face presently in our community? In your experience, what do you feel is needed to help our children and youth with the problems and unmet needs they experience? What difficulties exist that are barriers to providing help for these problems to our children and youth? What programs and staff does our community have that could be used to help resolve the problems and difficulties listed? Would you or a representative of your office be willing to attend a meeting of elected officials, agency representatives, and other individuals to discuss developing a community plan for serving children and youth? (See Figure 3-2.)

FIGURE 3–2
Program Information Sheet

---

1. NAME OF PROGRAM:

2. ADDRESS OF COMMUNITY:

3. PUBLICATION DESCRIBING PROGRAM:

4. PRINCIPLES UTILIZED:

5. GENERAL DESCRIPTION:

The information derived from the questions usually will cover all areas needed in the assessment phase. Any individual or agency who indicates an interest in participating in the planning process should be immediately invited to join the steering committee.

Selecting a Response System

The steering committee should examine results of similar projects in other communities to determine what types of programs have been successful and in what types of environments they have worked. The resources in Appendix A of this book contains selected examples. There are at least three criteria that need to be considered in evaluating programs that are examined. First, approaches must illustrate the use of broad concepts and address the multiple causes of behavior that are implied by the at-risk youth approach. Second, programs need to address the areas of concern identified by the community as problems. Third, the approaches are those that the community will accept if implemented.

Current approaches to suicide and risk prevention are varied and address many different strategies, with a wide range of results. For example, some schools limit their efforts to enlisting outside speakers who present dramatic descriptions of suicide and offer simplistic solutions to students in one-time presentations (Tugend, 1985). Others only offer crisis counseling after a death or other traumatic event (Robertson & Mathews, 1989), while early detection and treatment is stressed in another program (Blumenthal & Kupfer, 1988).

There are numerous comprehensive school based programs, some of which are widely known, such as those in Omaha, Nebraska; Plano, Texas; and New Jersey (Deaton & Morgan, 1992, p. 46). Curricula, such as the one developed in Wisconsin by the Department of Public Instruction (Berkan, 1990), also can be reviewed by the committee in order to be assured that there is an understanding of all components of the anticipated prevention plan. Each approach must be studied for those parts that will work in the community and become integrated into a program that fits local needs.

During 1985, Wisconsin Rapids, Wisconsin, experienced a series of youth suicides that devastated the community. Representatives of the school, the mental health clinic, the social service department, and a large private medical facility met to find ways to deal with the problem. As a group they followed the planning process described here and developed a training program for schools, businesses, community agency staff, and the general public. Training the participants in the physical and emotional needs of individuals, how to recognize depression and suicidal behavior, and how to refer students for help were all addressed. Community members were empowered to take positive action to provide prevention or intervention services to those individuals who needed assistance. Two results of the efforts were a dramatic reduction of suicides and the creation of a training manual based on their process (Coombs, 1990).

Building Support

In the previous steps, the steering committee explored the problem and the resources available, recruited committee members, and studied the methods for dealing with the problem. The material from the planning stages was assembled in report form and presented to those individuals and agencies who were interested. One strategy for the presentation was to invite potential supporters to a meeting in which the results of the work to that point were discussed. Prior to the meeting the participants were given a copy of the report and told that the final draft would include the results of the meeting. Following the meeting the draft was reviewed and changes agreed to in the meeting were included.

Designing the Plan

The information developed in the previous planning steps provides information to develop a model and strategy to deal with the problem that is workable for the community. The plan must include a clear description of the goals and methods of the plan, an integrated use of available resources, protocols to allow one agency to efficiently obtain the assistance of another, definitions of the role each agency and individual will play in the plan, and development of institutionalized methods by which the plan will be implemented and evaluated.

A basic starting point is to choose a limited number of goals that will be shared by all committee members. Objectives and activities are developed from the goals, and organizations and individuals are assigned to develop the activities. Timelines are set, and regular progress reports are made to the steering committee. An example of a key activity is the school's assignment of the review and revision of their suicide prevention/crisis intervention policy and procedures. In order to do so, committee members will need to have the assistance of the community agencies to reach interagency agreements covering class presentations, the response of staff or students to a death, assessment of potentially suicidal students, emergency transportation of suicidal students, and postvention activities. Mental health agencies may need to revise their approach to the school to include closer working relationships with troubled students.

Overall, the committee may decide to seek to enrich existing recreational and employment activities for youth as preventive measures. The agencies with experience in implementing the Job Training Partnership Act and other supportive employment programs are valuable resources that illustrate successful collaboration efforts among schools, community agencies, and businesses to enhance work experiences of youth.

It is the responsibility of each agency within the community to decide the extent of its participation in prevention plans within the scope of its available resources and legal mandate. Although the school provides part of the community plan, it must also have an internal plan of its own. A useful approach for developing the plan is to consider the school itself as a community with all its functions. There is a social structure, work responsibilities, and recreational opportunities that make up the fabric of the daily life of the school. All these functions are governed and coordinated by the administration and school board. As in any social organization, the success of the school depends on each individual and group accepting and playing appropriate roles. Administration must identify and attempt to meet the social, emotional, and educational needs of the students and the staff. Students must attend and cooperate with the educational efforts without disrupting the experience of others.

Three types of community based/school focused programs that include sound suicide prevention approaches are Broad Brush Student Assistance Program, At Risk, and Youth Services. A brief description of each follows.

Of the three, the Broad Brush Student Assistance Program is the most traditional (Berkan, 1990). It utilizes the existing alcohol and other drug abuse prevention program and adds suicide and crisis intervention to the basic services. Students are referred through the same process for suicidal crisis as for drug and alcohol problems. Many of the same community agencies are utilized to provide intervention and follow-up services to students. Because in many communities the resources needed to deal with the drug and alcohol and suicide problems are similar, the arrangement is a logical one. Obstacles that must be overcome involve restrictions on use of agency funds, training staff to work with students who may be suicidal as well as substance abusers, and informing students that the program is a resource for several related needs.

The youth at risk approach emphasizes the need to coordinate the school's educational mission with the intervention and treatment role of the community agencies. It is valuable in situations where the school and the community agencies have not traditionally coordinated their efforts for youth. The school concentrates on the identification of at-risk students, who are then referred to other community agencies for selected services. In cases in which agencies provide day treatment at off-school sites, the school provides the educational component for students in treatment (Berkan, 1990).

The youth at risk approach involves more joint planning by the school district, community agencies, businesses, and elected political representatives. It is a prevention program that involves identification of the extent of various youth problems (including suicide), evaluation of the extent and effectiveness of community resources, and study of the cause and remediation of the problem behaviors. After the extent of the youth problems is determined and school-community-family resources are assessed, a collaborative approach to resolving problems is developed. Agencies are expected to bring resources to the effort and engage in collaborative planning as determined by the team. Such efforts might be directed at developing youth recreation programs, economic opportunities, better housing, and reduction of violence and crime. These efforts are directed at enhancing the overall school and community climate in ways that will benefit youth. The assumption is that by so doing, youth will be able to cope better themselves and seek available help when needed. At its core the approach encourages a change in attitude between the adult population and youth from one characterized by distrust and fear to one that recognizes their mutual interdependence (Berkan, 1990).

An essential aspect of the plan is to establish criteria to measure its success. Youth risk behaviors such as suicide, alcohol and drug use, sexual activity, and gang activity should all be addressed by the plan. It would be a mistake, however, to base an evaluation of the success of the plan solely on whether the community experiences a reduction in youth risk behaviors. Evaluation should also include positive related outcomes, with students attending school more regularly, increasing their participation in community activities, and increasing the number of youth referrals to community programs for assistance.

Gaining Approval of the Plan

The individuals on the planning committee can keep key members of their constituency advised of the progress of the plan and incorporate their reactions and ideas into the final version. Each agency and group has an opportunity to review the latest draft of the plan and react to its content. Approval does not occur at a single point in time, but it is a process that defines an outcome acceptable to all concerned. In reality, action aimed at formalizing this step should never be taken until the committee is certain that there is consensus on major concerns and objections of the participating agencies and groups. Approval of the plan at this stage requires that the committee or an ally from each of the agencies and groups present the plan to the administration or governing board of each cooperator for their approval. Each group must be given the time and the support to explain the plan and seek approval through their governing boards. The plan requires commitment of resources and staff assignments, and there are legal implications that must be considered for each agency or group. An official approval process provides the participants an opportunity to give the plan a final review.

Implementing

The committee is a natural training group to present the content of the plan to the staff of the agencies and groups involved. Individuals on the committee become responsible for advising staff who have a role in the implementation of the plan in its operation. As representatives of the agencies and groups who are implementing the plan, committee members are in a strategic position to provide encouragement and technical assistance to the staff working with the plan. They also provide valuable feedback on the plan's operation to the steering committee.

Evaluating

The committee defines what they expect to achieve from the implementation of the plan and how that change will be measured. It is unrealistic to expect that all suicide and other risk behaviors will be totally eliminated by the new program. It is difficult to prove that certain activities of the plan prevented something from happening. However, evaluating several outcomes over a considerable time period can provide a comprehensive picture of results.

Evaluation targets should be simple, measurable, and jointly agreed upon by the committee. Examples might be increased numbers of youth referred for assistance to community agencies, increased number of self-referrals, specific number of crisis interventions performed as a result of the plan, increased knowledge of youth and other community members of available resources, statistical trends (over an extended period of time) of reduction of youth risk behaviors, and number of classroom and/or group presentations on topics related to the plan.

When planning the evaluation component, measures should be divided into at least two categories: those that can be measured in one year or less and those that must be measured over a longer period. An annual report of the effect of the plan can be used to maintain community support, redesign implementation, justify staff and funding requests, and provide decision makers with data for policy-making decisions.

4

Prevention

The purpose of public education is to help individuals acquire knowledge, skills, and positive attitudes toward self and others that will enable them to solve problems, think creatively, continue learning, and develop maximum potential for leading productive, fulfilling, lives in a complex and changing society.
— Minnesota Legislative Commission on Public Education, 1985

Just as effective education integrates many subjects and strives to relate them logically, prevention education dealing with death and violence within the school integrates three major areas of emphasis: curriculum, school climate, and community connections. Each of these areas addresses a specific aspect of influence on the lives of students. The curriculum provides information to the student within a context of instruction that encourages practical application of that information. The school climate includes all of the classroom instruction, staff-student relationships, student-student relationships, and extracurricular activities that occur within the context of the school experience. Community connections comprise all of the instructional experiences, collaborative programs, and services in which the school and the community cooperate to provide to students. Most importantly, connections are made with the families of students.

INFUSING AND REVISING THE CORE
CURRICULUM TO INCLUDE SELF-ESTEEM, STRESS
REDUCTION, AND PROBLEM-SOLVING SKILLS

Integrated instruction is a coordinated effort to teach several different topics in several related disciplines. Health topics can and should be included as units of instruction in disciplines such as science, home economics, and social studies. Likewise, reading, writing, speaking, and computation skills can and should be strengthened within the health instruction program. (Bradley, 1987, p. xi)

The educational community has increasingly recognized its responsibility to develop educational experiences for students that include factual information, training in skills, and attention to the affective components of the students' life experience. It is all done within an integrated curriculum approach.

In any curriculum, students are expected to master several competencies. They must learn enough information about an area to gain a basic understanding of the topic. They must identify how the information applies to them personally and how to use it effectively. They must use the information to understand and relate to others more effectively. They must learn how the information relates to the community beyond the school setting and how that knowledge may be used to help them function within the larger community (Bradley, 1987). The effectiveness of prevention programs for suicide and other youth risk behaviors is dependent on helping students master the four competencies. The extent to which students acquire competencies that increase social skills is related as much to the abilities and trustworthiness of adults as the ability of the students to learn this material (Nash, 1990).

Prevention information, such as that relating to suicide, is more effectively presented to students using the Socratic method than by a didactic approach. The teacher outlines the topic, provides basic, needed information, and allows the students to engage in a dialogue in which they teach one another. The teacher's command of the subject matter is important because it is the instructor who must ask the leading questions and guide students' understanding through a sharing of facts, opinions, and personal experiences. The Socratic method also provides the teacher with the opportunity to have a constant check on the level of factual knowledge, understanding, and practical application that students have achieved.

When the element of experiential education is included, students are able to understand the concepts of suicide prevention as it applies to them and their friends. An activity such as talking to other students about how to get help for depression and suicidal impulses has a strong impact on both the presenting and the listening student. Student assignments to study community resources provide them with an opportunity to visit community agencies that provide mental health and other services that people need at various times in their life.

The goals of a suicide prevention curriculum must include, at a minimum, basic information on the life and death cycle; facts about suicide, coping/helping skills, feelings, and interpersonal skills; and information about helping resources in the school and the community. Specific topics will include recognition and explanation of feelings, stress management, depression, emotional health, problem-solving techniques, communication skills, management of feelings, suicide warning signs, and how to seek help for self or a friend.

The curriculum should be age appropriate and build on the everyday experience of the students at home, in the school, and in the community. It is imperative that students learn ways to find support and assistance and ways to access formal and informal systems. More than any other message, it is central to suicide prevention that young people know there are adults who care and are dependable and that youth can find help by continuing to ask. One program that uses the concept effectively is the child protection training offered through the Wisconsin Committee for the Prevention of Child Abuse and Neglect (Flandreau-West, 1988). The program was developed to deal with the difficulty children have in recognizing that they are being abused and in asking a trusted adult for help in stopping the abuse. It uses a classroom venue to teach the children that they are not to blame for what adults do to them. The program helps the children recognize that their lives are filled with adults who care and helps them identify a helping network consisting of family members and other significant adults. Protective Behaviors, Inc., teaches children to also recognize, however, that when one adult in their network is not helpful, they should seek out another until help is received. Appendix A illustrates the content of an integrated suicide prevention curriculum developed by the Wisconsin Department of Public Instruction (Berkan, 1990, pp. 12–13).

A K–12 curriculum for suicide prevention does not contain specific units on suicide at each grade level. It strengthens the existing instructional units and brings specific information on suicide into the classroom at a time when students are developmentally ready to deal with the topic.

TOPICAL AREAS FOR DEATH EDUCATION IN SCHOOLS

There are six major topics for death education in the classroom curriculum. Each of the topics plays an important role in preparing the student to deal with the reality of life, death, and suicide.

Facts about Death and Dying

Factual information on death, dying, and suicide is clear cut and readily available. Current statistics from the American Association of Suicidology, the Center for Disease Control in Atlanta, and the state government health agencies form the foundation of this presentation. Information such as death rates for specific age cohorts, homicide rates, accidental deaths, and suicide rates are included. Materials that deal with death and how to present it to students include descriptions of how health care professionals help patients and their families deal with death (Durham & Weiss, 1992; Hammer et al., 1992; Gifford & Cleary, 1990; Parkman, 1992).

Examples of appropriate practical topics included in the curriculum are life expectancy and causes of death, wills, organ donations, funeral customs and costs, and suicide trends. The classroom discussion of these topics provides students with the basis for dispelling myths and provides accurate information students often lack. With a factual knowledge base, children and youth are better able to incorporate other learning about death issues that is developmentally appropriate. It is a paradox that, in order to live rationally and fully, individuals must understand and accept their own inevitable death and that of others. Death education has as its goals to provide accurate information to students, increase their self-awareness of how the information relates to them, and increase their ability to deal with death as a natural part of life (Corr & McNeil, 1986).

Youth suicide represents a dramatic reason to include information about death within the school curriculum. Suicidologists cite the developmental confusion of youths regarding death and their incomplete understanding of death's finality as one of the factors in youth suicide (Berkan, 1990; Pfeffer, 1986; Jacobs, 1971; Kirk, 1993). Factual information can be valuable in making the concept of suicide and other causes of death real to students. Death education presents one way in which the educator can dispel myths about death and increase the students' understanding of death's finality (Corr & McNeil, 1986).

Suicide prevention education is an appropriate avenue within the school to utilize the knowledge of death educators to address a serious problem. Training materials, now available, have comprehensive, accurate descriptions of what is known about the causes of suicide and how to stop it. Frequently, these resources also have elaborate case studies as a part of their explanations (Berkan, 1990; Jacobs, 1971; American Association of Suicidology, 1981). A complete guide that includes a full curriculum, training for teachers, and a student workbook is found in *Dimensions of Loss and Death Education*, third edition (1992), by Patricia Zalaznik (see Sources section for ordering information).

Self-Esteem

Self-esteem may be defined as the sum total of what individuals think of themselves that leads them to assign value to their existence (Berkan, 1990). Every classroom teacher has the opportunity to help each student understand that they have intrinsic worth. Inherent personal value cannot be effected by achievement alone but occurs because individuals are concerned about others and learn how to use their innate abilities to function effectively. Self-esteem is tied to students' understanding and ability to judge themselves on how well they use their abilities and not on whether their abilities are as good as or better than others. Students who develop healthy self-esteem know that they have attributes that others can admire just as they appreciate attributes others have. Classroom teachers at all levels can provide opportunities for students to experience an affirmation of themselves by recognizing their accomplishments and their positive characteristics as part of regular classroom activities.

Feelings and Emotions

Feelings are emotional states that individuals experience as a result of events that happen in their lives (Berkan, 1990). It is critical that students be given help in learning how to deal with the feelings and emotions they experience. Whether that emotion is love or anger, young people need to know how to express and handle it appropriately. Youth are beginning to develop experience in recognizing strong emotions and are frightened by many of the intense feelings they experience. Through literature and through sharing their own adult feelings with students, teachers, and other significant adults, students are able to model how these intense experiences can be mastered. It is important that the feelings of the student be recognized as legitimate and not discounted while at the same time giving the message that life is filled with events that seem over-whelming at the time. It is helpful for students to learn that disappoint-ment and discouragement happen to everyone and that we have control over many of our feelings and actions. Perhaps the biggest lesson students must learn is that life goes on; pain now is real, but, in time, it is replaced with pleasure and excitement again. In suicide-proofing individuals, it is important to let them know that they have a future to look forward to that has meaning and satisfaction.

Coping

Life is not a well laid out set of experiences but instead presents a series of choices that have consequences, and each brings with it pleasure or pain. The task of each individual is to learn how to make good choices and to deal with the result of choices that do not work out (Berkan, 1990).

Youth have not yet developed a life experience base from which to develop many coping strategies. Significant adults are responsible to be available to young people to talk to them, to explain what works and what does not, to suggest alternative decisions, and to help them cope with the results of bad decisions. It is critical for youth to learn that an individual does not have to succeed at everything they attempt if they are to develop successful coping skills.

Students need to be taught that it is acceptable to move away from situations that are getting out of their control and that it is not possible to be a superperson who can solve all the problems right away. It is important to teach youth that some problems solve themselves and that some problems have no solutions and that withdrawing temporarily is often the only way to tell which is which. Being able to change how one is attempting to solve a problem (redirection) is another category youth often miss because they do not realize that there can be many solutions to a problem. Students can see that they need not settle for failure but can change tactics. One student observed "It's like saying you are never defeated because you just postpone your victories." Sometimes students need to know that it is best to compromise and redefine (reevaluate) their goals. Although it may mean settling for less than they originally wanted, it may be more than they can get any other way.

Confrontation is an important skill students need to learn in terms of confronting their own tendency to avoid problems. Students can reduce the effect of fear or an attack by another person by facing the problem and not allowing it to grow larger through avoiding it. It is a skill that can be talked about in class but must be practiced in everyday life to be of value and to become a part of responses to problems. Concerned adults who are available and approachable as needed by students are the key to learning about coping mechanisms.

Locating and Giving Help

The hopeless feeling that is part of developing a suicidal state of mind comes in part from the failure of an individual to understand that there are people and agencies who can help resolve problems that are overwhelming when faced alone. One of the tragic consequences of a suicide is that those around the deceased could have helped but did not know how or that their help was needed. Most people learn where and when to ask for help through trial and error, and for some, that ability could have interrupted their self-destructive behavior (Berkan, 1990).

Curricular materials that describe the help, how to get it, and when to ask for it teach important preventive skills to students. Students can conduct interviews with school and community agency staff and then report to the rest of the class as a practical way to introduce them to the skill of seeking help. Additional information about teachers, parents, social workers, doctors, psychologists, and nurses flows easily and naturally into introducing community agencies into the class as students mature. Throughout the sequence, the fact that help is available can become second nature to the individual and aids in the defense against self-destruction.

Suicide and Depression

Suicide and depression are concepts that are not easy for students to understand, and, therefore, the initial presentation of them is delayed until the students have matured enough to understand their implications. Instruction usually occurs at sixth or seventh grade because it is the age cohort where suicides begin to increase in frequency in children (Jackson, 1966; Corr & McNeil, 1990; Berkan, 1990; Pfeffer, 1986; Curran, 1987). It is important to include information that shows the linkage between suicidal behavior and alcohol and drug abuse. Information should include how to recognize the signs of these conditions and when to offer or seek help for them (Berkan, 1990; Pfeffer, 1989; Davidson & Linnoila, 1991). A factual, direct approach designed not to frighten but to inform students is important. Presentations about suicide should always be given in small groups and in time periods that will allow the students to process the material (Ross, 1985). Usually, the signs that warn of suicidal risk are stressed, but this must not be done without also reiterating the help that is available. Children and youth need to know the limits of their responsibility for suicidal and violent peers, and treating and stopping dangerous behavior is primarily an adult obligation. It gives the students a direction for their concern that is positive and can result in prevention of a suicide or other destructive act.

Life Plan

A teaching unit on life planning for young adults can include suicide prevention. It begins with statistics that show a significant increase in young adult suicide during the period two to three years after graduating from high school. It appears that suicidal young adults were able to function in the school setting because they had a natural support system of friends and staff available to them during crisis. After graduation, they were forced to develop new support systems (Berkan, 1990). High school friends go elsewhere to school or to jobs, and young persons are frequently left without enough support to meet their needs as they are challenged to develop a more independent life (Erikson, 1968). The life plan unit in high school concentrates on students becoming familiar with the community resources and the manner of accessing them. It builds on the knowledge acquired over 12 years of schooling to have the student make future plans about work, recreation, or schooling after high school in such a way to anticipate problems and know at least one or two ways to deal with them.

DEVELOPING CURRICULUM UNITS ON DEATH, DYING, AND GRIEVING

Successful instruction in suicide prevention includes the educational instruction skills of teachers and the mental health skills of school social workers, psychologists, nurses, and counselors. Each professional group has specific types of skills that can be used in the development of death, dying, and grieving units for students. In addition to in-school staff, the community agencies dealing with mental health, child welfare, and family services have staff who possess skills that can be used by educators in the development and presentation of suicide prevention materials to students. All of these professionals can contribute ideas and concepts and can review the curriculum content for accuracy in order to insure that the most accurate information is included. Use of organized parent groups such as parent-teacher organizations and church groups and concerned parents as curriculum advisors and reviewers can avoid many misunderstandings and fears on the part of everyone concerned with the welfare of the students. Although it is valuable for others to review the content of the curriculum, the professional educators' expertise in organizing the material and choosing the method of presentation is critical in the actual delivery.

CLIMATE

The family and the school are the two most important environments for the development of the students' emotional and psychological well-being. Each of these strong influences supports the other, and each has a unique role to play. Families are the primary source of moral instruction and are the socially responsible institution charged with the development of children in our society.

However, schools share the responsibility for guiding children because they are responsible for providing a safe and nurturing environment. During each school day the educational setting becomes the source of protection and growth. The educational staff are responsible for the safety and development of the children in their care. They must create an atmosphere that is appropriate to the age and developmental stage of the child (Wehlage, Rutter, Smith, & Lesko 1989). In creating a developmental climate in the schools the following are principles to consider.

Students Are Seeking Transitions into Adult Life

At times, students will act very mature and will seem to understand their responsibilities and the consequences of their actions. At other times, they will appear to have regressed to an earlier stage of development and will act in a manner that is irresponsible and unacceptable to the adults in their environment. This is a critical factor to keep in mind, because it requires special response from the adults. Creation of a nurturing school climate means that, although appropriate consequences are administered, the student must not be made to feel that immature actions lessens their acceptance as worthwhile individuals by adults in the school. School professionals must realize that young people are looking to them for a reaffirmation of their worth as individuals, and rejection by the significant adults in the school will mean that the developing self-esteem of the student may be damaged severely. Clear and fair disapproval of an action and administration of consequences followed by reassurance of continued respect is central to the positive learning experience and development of a strong sense of self.

Discipline Should Lead to Positive Growth

Self-esteem and social skill development are built on the cumulative experiences of learning what not to do and receiving approval for appropriate actions. The Children's Trust Fund, a child abuse prevention organization with affiliates in all 50 states, has a program entitled "Catch Your Kid Doing Something Good" as a means of reducing the risk of child abuse by directing adults to notice the positive things a child does rather than their mistakes, thereby encouraging children to try harder in a positive way. In the school setting, youth can grow when they realize that adults like them as persons first and see them as students who must meet performance standards second.

There are times when student behaviors are so negative that the school must take action to change the situation, but the impact of denial of privileges must be carefully weighed in relation to the individual child. Students who have few activities at school from which they receive positive recognition or feelings of belonging may be heavily invested in such activities as sports or drama and will be disproportionately punished if they are prevented from participating. Before assessing penalties, it is well to consider what those activities mean to the student and whether other alternatives might be more effective. If students have few positive influences in their lives, some other consequence should be considered.

The use of differential discipline is key to protecting the self-esteem of students and supporting the goal of preventing self-destructive behaviors, including suicide, in individuals (Wolfe, 1993).

Students Should Be Encouraged to Develop Pride in the School Environment

In order for individuals to develop a sense of self, they must also experience a positive identification with the environment in which they function. As students realize their ability to affect the world around them, they gain a sense of self-control and are less likely to develop feelings of helplessness that can lead to depression and suicide.

The environment within the classroom should reflect the cumulative interests of the students who are in the class. Much as the selection of items on the door of the refrigerator in many homes becomes a window into the activities of the family, the bulletin boards and the walls of the classroom are displays of what is important to the class members, both as individuals and as a group. For a student to see others enjoying what they have accomplished or what they find interesting is a reaffirmation of their individual worth. The classroom teacher's task is to provide appropriate positive feedback for all students. In later years, especially in high school, the shift is toward other-directed behavior, such as encouraging students to select and acknowledge the work of others and to maintain the physical appearance and the behavioral standards of the school itself as well.

The development of a school climate conducive to suicide and violence prevention would include activities such as developing behavioral codes, organizing clean up campaigns of the buildings and grounds, and planning extracurricular activities. Students, as individuals and as groups, can exert change through positive means in projects they have helped design and accomplish. The experience gained by their efforts shows that success can come from persistent work and that the efforts of all members are valued.

Adult Mentors Are Essential for Students

The value of the experiences provided within the school setting will not be enough by themselves for all students. When they feel that they are being rejected and discounted by peers or adults in the school, students need the reassurance of other adults who will realize the importance of continuing support and encouragement. The mentor provides unconditional support and acts as an advocate for the student. Mentors are active in seeking out specific students and checking on their experience in and out of the school setting. Mentoring insures that the normal reticence of students to ask for help does not prevent them from being helped. There are two categories of mentors: those who are assigned by formal action of the school and those who are natural mentors. All students in a school should be assigned mentors at the beginning of their school experience, and mentors should maintain long-term relationships with their students. Traditional school counselor assignments, or student advisors, usually do not function as mentors; their functions are more directed toward the academic and administrative needs of the school rather than the developmental needs of the students. Natural mentors are chosen by the students themselves in the normal course of school life. Adult-student relationships develop around shared experiences in and out of the classroom. An individual student may choose more than one natural mentor in a given year or from year to year. Each mentor fulfills a function for the student, and different mentors may be selected when a function is completed and the student moves on to another set of activities.

As a direct result of a series of youth suicides in Plano, Texas, the school district instituted a mentor system that was available to all students but focused on those thought to be at risk of suicide. Peer mentors were assigned to keep track of new students and to help them adjust to their new school environment. Adult mentors checked on an assigned group of students on a regular basis to monitor their emotional health. The message to students was that they were not alone and that someone cared who was interested in helping them solve their daily problems (American Association of Suicidology, 1987).

COMMUNITY CONNECTIONS

Traditionally, schools have developed unique internal social structures that provide services to students designed to help them achieve success in the educational setting while taking care not to supplant the role of either the family or the community. In order to best serve the individual student in the family, school, and community environments, it is necessary to provide formal and informal ties among all three elements. Intervention strategies described in Chapter 6 are ways that schools can develop effective communications with families and community agencies. Developing a referral system insures that the noninstructional needs of students are met through appropriate community services.

Family, school, and community agencies must understand that when they interact around the needs of a student, they are constructing a meaningful picture of the student's adjustment and needs within the total environment of children called youth. Schools must be able to communicate the strengths and weaknesses of the individual student and describe what they can offer to be of assistance. Parents must be able to recognize that proposed services are appropriate for their children. In instances where the school procedures or structure may be creating the problems, the assessment of the parents must be valued in determining remedial action taken by the school. Community agencies are limited by their missions as to the services they may provide. In addition, budgetary constraints are realistic considerations that must be factored into the establishment of a service plan for students.

A collaborative approach, based on clear communication, assumes that several factors are present. First, families, schools, and community all have valuable resources to share. Second, all three entities have resources that vary from time to time based on budget, time, and the needs of students. Third, all three entities have their own agendas and viewpoints and may sometimes respond in a defensive manner that hinders collaborative programming. Collaboration consists of all parties bringing resources to the table to be shared with others involved in the programming. It infers that all parties will agree on the goals needed to assist the student and the method of delivering services and will share the credit or responsibility for the outcome of the effort. It is essential to remove arbitrary barriers, such as not allowing community agencies or parents access to the school or refusing to meet parents except during normal school or business hours. In some cases it is necessary to remove barriers through advocating legislative or school board policy change.

The most often ignored task in the school plan is the development of effective referral procedures for community services. Representatives from schools, community agencies, and parents should meet to reduce to writing a definition of appropriate roles; a description of the actions that can be expected from all parties; an understanding of the limits of service and appropriate involvement with which all parties must deal; and a detailed agreement of how to refer for service, what service will be provided, and who will provide it. Although all parents cannot be involved in this process, representatives of parents from all ethnic and socioeconomic groups in the community need to participate.

Integrating the elements appropriate to the school, to the community, and to the family provides the maximum effect on the prevention of completed youth suicide and provides a nurturing, protective atmosphere for children and youth for positive growth.

EVALUATING SCHOOL ACTIVITIES FOR PARTICIPATION AND COMPETITIVE VALUES

Prevention efforts can be enhanced by developing skills, resiliency, and self-confidence through a blend of competitive and participatory activities in the school. Academic and extracurricular activities in schools are, by nature, designed to enhance skill through competition or develop the student's ability to function with others through participation and cooperation. Refining existing efforts, rather than developing new school programs, holds more promise not only for cost-effective reasons but also because many have negative effects on some students that require changes before their prevention potential can be realized. Highly competitive programs that allow only small numbers of the most proficient and committed students to participate help those youth achieve their best and learn how to focus sustained efforts toward reaching important goals. Youth also learn how to function effectively as members of a group or team activity and to enjoy the association of others in a common enterprise.

On the negative side, participants in highly competitive activities may devalue themselves when they do not win, refuse to take part in any activity where they cannot excel, or learn inappropriately aggressive ways to physically or psychologically injure others to gain advantage (Martens, 1978). Among the competitive activities to be carefully evaluated are varsity sports, band and orchestra, cheerleading, student council, and science fairs.

Highly competitive activities, which limit student participation to those with the highest motivation and most advanced skill potential, often become the standard of acceptable achievement for all students. In schools where only the few most skilled become the standard that all must seek to emulate, other students who do not have the ability to excel in one of the valued arenas develop poor self-images and fail to use their unique abilities. In designing school programs that are competitive but that also value participation and cooperation, planners must consider a hierarchy that is based on a choice of both the level of competition and a comprehensive selection of activities.

The categories of competition can be divided into recreational, intramural, and interscholastic. The recreational level of competition provides an opportunity for students to try new activities in search of what interests them. At times the student may find both an interest and an ability that can lead them to a higher level of competition. In other situations the student's ability or desire to handle the level of competition may remain low, but the benefits that the student derives from association with peers has the same positive value as that gained by students functioning at higher competitive levels. Intramural competition can also occur in athletics, academics, or recreational interest areas. It is characterized by activities that meet the needs of students with intermediate skills in a given area and a desire to test those abilities against other students. Intramural competition can become an end in itself or a way for students to pursue the possibilities of achieving at a higher level. It provides a lower risk setting for students to experiment with the possibility that they can achieve more than they or others might realize at first. If they find they cannot progress further, they are not subject to having publicly failed to reach the highest level of competition. Often overlooked at this level is the spectrum of activities that students are able to use to discover areas in which they have talent. Students often find that they are able to achieve in many areas, though not at the highest level. A combination of opportunities for interests and achievement to flourish can help them become well-rounded, interesting, successful persons who are better prepared for the challenges of adult life.

Participation activities include intramural games, science or foreign language clubs, peer counseling groups, student newspapers, school annuals, plays, talent shows, and clubs. Projects in such areas as school fund raising and community betterment also provide cooperative participation experiences for students.

Some activities involve joint efforts by school and community groups. The Key Clubs for high school students by Kiwanis and patriotic speech competitions by the American Legion are two examples found in most urban and rural school districts.

Experts in children's sports programs cite their experience and research that indicates children and youth do not perceive winning and losing in the same way as adults: "Children often define success in terms of trying one's best, improving since the last performance and enjoying the activity. The process of mastering and demonstrating skills rather than the product . . . is deemed most important by children and youth" (Weirs, 1989).

David Elkind's (1981) work is probably best known among many experts who have commented about parents and other adults who push children into highly competitive activity out of their own needs. The parent who wants his or her eight year old to perform like a professional football player or concert pianist is altogether too familiar to teachers and school counselors. Such children may react by becoming very aggressive or obsessively fearful of failure or being second best. Neither outcome develops resilient, productive, or confident children and youth.

There has been more written about negative consequences from sports than other competitive activities in the schools, but any organized, competitive activity that restricts participation to a small number of the very best performers among children should be scrutinized.

Activities should be evaluated through periodic administrative reviews. Faculty meeting agendas can include discussion of the effectiveness and appropriateness of cooperative and competitive student activities. Student councils can be challenged to provide student reviews and inputs. The opinions and experience of parents can also be utilized in determining the comprehensive nature and the effectiveness of school activities for students.

Involvement of faculty and students in evaluating the effects of the school experience on students is consistent with current school reform movements that include stakeholders in the design and evaluation of the school program (Fullan & Stiegelbauer, 1991; Villa et al., 1992).

The authors suggest a set of questions and guidelines for evaluating school programs.

Questions for Guided Discussion

Are the intended goals for participation and for competition clear to students and faculty?

Is there the anticipated level of participation and interest by students in the activity?

If participation is more or less than anticipated, have efforts been made to discover why?

What indicators of commitment and enthusiasm are there by students?

Is there evidence of growth in skills or task accomplishment in student participants?

Are students more able to collaborate or cooperate with others to accomplish tasks or goals as a result of their participation over time?

Do faculty, coaches, or other adult sponsors have sufficient time to plan and engage with students effectively in the activity? Do adult leaders perform appropriately in terms of promoting both developmental and competitive goals?

Guidelines for Evaluating Projects and Activities in the Schools

The goals for the activity should be clearly stated in terms of their intended effects on the student.

Examples: If a practical or technical skill such as reading music, playing a sports position, or performing an engine repair is the goal, what provision is there for learning and then practicing the skill? If learning to cooperate with others is a goal, what opportunity is there to plan and carry out a group activity successfully?

The extent to which the activity is inclusive rather than exclusive in numbers of students served should be possible to verify or estimate.

Examples: Are as many students as possible involved in managing, writing, reporting, and advertising in the school newspaper and annual? Do school publications have stories and pictures involving a wide variety of subjects and people?

The allocation of resources of money, staff, and time for their balance and fit with the mission of the school can be examined.

Examples: Major varsity sports are expensive relative to any other noninstructional activity; basketball, in particular, uses a small number of players of the same sex, as contrasted to a track team, which can utilize many student athletes of both sexes with a variety of individualized skills.

The amount and quality of adult influence and control of the program and its goals requires careful analysis. Because adults control the resources and leadership of most activities, the opportunity for student involvement is not regularly examined.

Examples: Prevention program agendas for suicide, drug and alcohol abuse, and pregnancy are so totally adult dominated that the adults do not often consider whether they are producing the intended effects with children and youth (Melaville & Blank, 1993, pp. 17–18). In some local communities, aggressive adult groups interested in sports activities or morality positions exert questionable influences on students and schools.

Several guides are available to assist schools in planning and evaluating organized sports and other activities. *Guidelines for Children's Sports* (1979) by Rainer Martens and Vern Seefeldt is a useful example.

IN-SERVICE TRAINING TO UNDERSTAND AND TEACH DEATH, GRIEF, AND LOSS ISSUES

In-service training represents an integral part of a comprehensive suicide and other death issues education program. Suicide prevention training in schools provides an example of how similar programs can be designed so that staff in community agencies, parents of students in the school, and school staff can take part.

In suicide prevention training, it is advisable to provide different training sessions for professionals, other staff, and parents. Those professionals who will be assigned direct responsibility to implement the suicide prevention curriculum and prevention program will receive more specialized training. There will be separate training for parents and other staff persons.

The training workshops for both groups should contain the following topics at a minimum:

Statistical description of the problem in the district, community, and state.

Background information, which would include a historical perspective on how society has dealt with suicide. This allows the audience to begin to understand the taboo nature of the topic as it relates to religious, legal, and social views.

Representatives of the legal, religious, and mental health community can review the material to insure that it is factual and represents diverse community interests. The role of these individual representatives is not to censor material or dictate how it will be taught. The suicide and death issues training for professional educators and counselors who will implement the prevention curriculum and services plan of the school will include a compilation of the myths and facts of suicide and the warning signs and behavioral indicators of a student in suicidal crisis.

The relationship of alcohol and other drug abuse to teen suicide.

Effective intervention techniques, including initial assessment of risk.

Effective referral procedures to community agencies, including working with the parents to insure the successful referral for further assessment and/or treatment.

Reintegrating the suicidal student back into the school setting after treatment.

Local needs and experience of presenters may suggest other areas to be covered to tailor training to local needs. Developing a prevention plan in collaboration with other local organizations, parents, and students holds great promise for the future in preventing deaths and permanent injuries among children and youth. It encourages a shift in the thinking of the school and community toward positive growth of its youth and prevention of harm and violence rather than waiting to respond only when there is a crisis. Finally, when the community responds with actions that show that it genuinely cares for the lives, safety, and growth of its children, most students will respond positively in a newly created atmosphere of hope and favorable possibilities.

5

Intervention

Daniel Morgan

Intervention approaches and models appropriate for use by teachers and staff within the school setting and collaboration with other community agencies and parents provide the focus for intervention plans and activities.

In a general sense, intervention includes all efforts designed to prevent suicide and other destructive behavior. Intervention activities include developing general school policies and procedures for handling suicide attempts; recognizing signs and symptoms of emotional instability, self-destructive thoughts, and suicidal behavior; providing immediate crisis response and psychological first aid to reduce and prevent suicidal thoughts and behavior in teens; assessing the level of appropriate intervention; engaging parents and peers; and referring, reintegrating, and monitoring the student returning to the school setting.

Intervention in teen suicide within the school setting differs from assessment and treatment of other types of personal problems related to students because of the immediate and continuous response required to prevent lethal, irreversible acts of completed suicidal behavior. We have characterized suicide as the preventable death, and it is often true that many youths will choose to live if they can be helped through current troubles they are experiencing.

SCHOOL POLICY AND PROCEDURES

Prevention of suicide in the school setting is an ongoing process that must be given administrative sanction through written policy and procedural guidelines, developed specific to interventions, that are continuously reviewed and updated. Ogden and Germanario (1988, pp. 111–18) suggest the following general school policies and set of procedures that are comprehensive and can be adapted to most school settings for handling suicide attempts.

Procedural guidelines must be established for handling situations that may result in self-inflicted harm.

All potential suicide situations must be reported to the principal and school counselor.

Staff will be held harmless for reporting information on potential suicide of a student.

Staff cannot be required to guarantee confidentiality. Even if it was promised, the responsibility is to share needed information with appropriate others, including administrative staff, parents, and anyone providing treatment for the suicide attempt.

The school has the responsibility to gather information from the student, and others, concerning a possible suicide.

If the student is at extreme high risk, a staff member should remain with the student.

A suicidal student should not be allowed to leave school until a safety plan is assured.

Parents have the right to know when their child is at risk, and they have the primary responsibility to provide for any treatment.

The school has responsibility for ongoing support of a student at risk within the limits of its resources and mission.

Parents and treatment agencies can count on the cooperation of the school in assisting the child at risk.

Of all the suggested policies and procedures listed by Ogden and Germanario, the issues surrounding confidentiality cause the most problems for school administrators and staff. The American Psychological Society (1989, pp. 390–95) has developed legal and ethical guidelines that cover circumstances in which confidentiality must be broken. In essence, a person's confidentiality is protected regardless of age, except in circumstances in which there is clear and eminent danger to self or others. The potentially suicidal child or youth provides a clear instance where client/patient confidentiality is to be broken because of serious potential danger. Also, parents have the legal right to any and all information obtained in an assessment or report of possible danger concerning their child (Brewer & Faitok, 1989, pp. 142–47). It is not necessary to divulge every personal statement or bit of information to the parents or others. Only appropriate information will be shared with parents or treatment agents, and it will be limited to those who have an absolute right to know for the protection and safety of the youth and effective further intervention in the matter.

RECOGNIZING SIGNS AND SYMPTOMATOLOGY

Adolescence is the period of growth between childhood and adulthood when young people are growing and changing physically, emotionally, and intellectually. Establishing an identity, achieving personal independence, choosing a career, and developing important relationships are milestones that adolescents usually face during this time. This difficult period is amplified because of growing independence from the family as a supportive network, increasing mobility, and the influences of peer pressure.

That adolescence is a difficult and troublesome time is reflected in the number of suicide attempts among children and adolescents. A number of studies report that as many as 10 percent of high school students have made at least one suicide attempt during their young lives, and one-third to one-half say they have thought about suicide as a means of dealing with their unresolved feelings (*Journal of School Health*, 1991, p. 439).

It is helpful to identify some common myths with facts concerning suicide:

Myth: Youths who talk about suicide will not actually attempt it.
Fact: It is estimated that over 80 percent of the youths who commit suicide give repeated warnings. Threats and suicidal talk are a warning cry for help that should not be ignored.
Myth: Suicidal youths actually want to die.
Fact: Most youths who are suicidal do not want to die; they want the emotional pain associated with their feelings of hopelessness, lack of significance, or inability to change the situation to go away so they can go on living as before.
Myth: Youths who attempt suicide once will not try again.
Fact: Four out of five people who kill themselves have attempted to do so at least once previously. After the barrier between thinking and acting is

crossed, it is easier to try a second or third time, especially if feelings about life have not changed and new coping skills have not been learned.

Myth: If you talk to a youth about suicide, it will give him or her ideas.

Fact: Suicidal youth already have the idea; by someone talking to them, they may feel relieved that someone finally recognizes their emotional pain. (Giffin & Felsenthal, 1983)

Although there is no typical suicidal youth, there are certain character-istics and situations that are important to know. Generally, suicidal behavior is an extreme form of communication in which the person desperately needs to feel loved and worthwhile. The individual also may be saying that something needs to be changed for life to continue to be worth living and that the person is powerless to act on the need.

Many young people engaged in suicidal activity want to be helped but have difficulty asking adults for assistance. A strong, perceptive adult can be of assistance to a suicidal youth by reaching out to determine what needs to be done to bring a change to the current life situation that seems unresolvable to the youth.

Suicidal youth tend to be ambivalent toward living. It appears that they have fallen out of love with life but are not ready to embrace death. Therefore, it is not unusual to find suicidal youth planning or doing something harmful to themselves while at the same time sending messages for help.

There are three words that begin with the letter H that characterize the dynamics of suicide. The first is the word "hopelessness." Although hope is figuratively the light at the end of the tunnel that people can see most of the time, suicidal people do not see alternative possibilities. One of the authors in training sessions describes hopelessness as the color black. Suicidal people often describe their situations as being black, or without hope for improvement. It is important to gently emphasize the concept of hope and pose alternatives to what is seen as a hopeless situation when dealing with suicidal thoughts of youth.

The second H is the word "helplessness." Suicidal youth are likely to view themselves as helpless to change their situations, which they also view as hopeless. Suicidal thought processes cause youth to begin to see the world with a tunnel vision perspective. The ability to look at obvious alternatives becomes perceptively constricted. An adult can help point out alternatives to alleviate emotional pain and alter the current life situation that the youth has been unable to perceive alone.

The third H is "haplessness." Many youth come from life situations in which lack of basic support and nurturing is the overwhelming life descriptor. Difficulties within the family such as poverty, divorce, violence, child neglect, or substance abuse are debilitating factors to suicide-prone youth.

Another important concept about suicidal thought in youth is suicidal erosion, which is the result of gradually wearing away the ability to cope with emotional pain. The young person's ability to deal with anger, loss, and disappointment is diminished. Often, youth who have not been taught healthy coping skills will react by running away or turning to alcohol or drugs to alleviate their turmoil. The result is further distancing from sources of the problem. Although the act of suicide may take only a split second, as in pulling the trigger of a gun, the process that results in the lethal action occurs over an extended period.

Fortunately, there are many clues and warning signals to suicide, and a high percentage of young people in suicidal crises will give notice of their intentions through warning signals. Some children will purposely present clues hoping someone will understand and rescue them, while others provide signs indirectly through their behavior. A teen may appear fatigued and irritable from depression that disrupts eating and sleeping habits. Others may present overt warning signs to test whether anyone around them really cares if they are dead or alive. One danger signal alone may not mean that there is suicidal intent, but a cluster of warning signals following recent loss, disappointment, grief, or similar emotionally troubling reactions is important (Hoff, 1991, pp. 126–28).

There are five major categories of suicide warning signs: verbal threats of suicide; previous suicide attempt(s); significant depression characterized by expressions of sadness, discouragement, or hopelessness; abrupt changes in behavior or personality; and giving away valued possessions.

Although substance abuse does not cause suicide, alcohol contributes significantly in over 46 percent of attempts by lowering impulse control and intensifying depression (Frymier, 1992, p. 108).

There are four categories of suicide indicators that can be observed by counselors and teachers. They include behavioral, verbal, situational, and affective areas (Deaton & Morgan, 1992, pp. 27–28).

Behavioral Indicators
Previous attempts
Decline in school performance
Giving away prized possessions
Withdrawing from others
Physical fighting with family members

Running away
Violent temper outbursts
Writing a diary about the desirability of death
Infatuation with media that glorify death as a solution to life problems in such
    forms as poetry, drawings, music, or satanic ritual
Extreme risk-taking behaviors
Games in which participants are required to assume fantasy identities and carry
    out heroic or deadly actions
Unresolved past experience with death
Rebellious behavior that is unusual for the person
Quietly putting affairs in order
Neglect of personal appearance
Increasing use of drugs or alcohol
Sexual promiscuity that has not been typical before

Verbal Indicators
Direct
    "I've decided to kill myself."
    "I wish I were dead."
    "Sometimes she makes me so mad I feel like killing myself."
    "I hate my life and everything about it."
    "I just can't go on any longer."
    "Life has lost all its meaning for me."
    "I've had it, life isn't worth living."
Indirect
    "Everyone would be better off without me."
    "I just can't deal with this anymore."
    "If I don't see you again, thanks for everything."
    "I'm not the person I used to be."
    "I think I've lived long enough to see what I'm to do."
    "Do you know the procedures for donating your eyes after death?"
    "I wish I could tell you how important you've been. Now I know the only
        way open for me."
    "Here, take my [cherished possession]; I won't be needing it soon."

Situational Indicators
Loss of an important relationship
Loss of an overvalued aspect of life (example: not becoming a cheerleader, not
    making the football team, not getting perfect grades)
Divorce of parents
Violence within the family
Violence with peers
Parent or school overemphasis on achievement
Social isolation from peers

Recent death of a friend
Living away from the family for the first time
Extended physical illness without recovery
Period following a long bout with depression
Suicide in extended family

Affective Indicators
Extreme self-criticism
Apathy
Recent weight loss or weight gain
Sleeplessness or oversleeping
Loss of pleasure or interest in activities
Lethargy
Becoming easily agitated
Feeling worthless
Feeling hopeless
Easily discouraged
Unable to concentrate or stay on task
Low frustration tolerance
Dwelling on problems
Living in the past
Social withdrawal
Indecisiveness
Focusing on failure
Ideas of self-punishment
Extreme despondency or euphoria
Lack of goal orientation
Exaggerated fears
Reduced ability to express affection
Feelings of being an undue burden to others
Lack of investment in the future

At some time or other in the lives of most people, a few of the signs and symptoms are present. However, a suicidal person will most often present a cluster of indicators in the context of a profound sense of sadness and hopelessness that lasts over time. To assess the seriousness of the situation presented, several questions should be answered: How intense are the feelings or behaviors? How long have the symptoms occurred? What portion of the young person's time is occupied with the symptomatic behavior? Is the observed behavior and expression of feeling typical for the student?

The greater the intensity, the longer the situation has lasted, and the more frequent the behaviors or expression of feelings, the more accurate are the indicators. Successful prevention of suicidal occurrence comes from observing the patterns of indicators and intervening directly before an actual attempt is made.

Of all the signs and symptoms, the single most critical warning is a previous attempted suicide.

IMMEDIATE CRISIS RESPONSE

Professional educators and school staff have humanitarian and legal responsibilities to safeguard students' health. Students are in school six to seven hours a day, and teachers and other staff are in an excellent position to identify students who are at risk.

If students threaten or show signs of being suicidal, immediate action in dealing with the crisis could make the difference between life and death.

The authors believe that teachers and staff can effectively respond to the potentially suicidal youth by providing a combination of brief psychological first aid and supportive confrontation. Teachers and other school staff have little time available for extra counseling; therefore, our suggestions are made in the context of using, in an effective manner, the time that will usually be expended anyway to deal with student crisis. The purpose of psychological first aid is to mobilize the coping abilities of the youth as quickly as possible, and it may be accomplished through several actions: making psychological contact, clarifying the problem, examining possible solutions, taking action, and establishing follow-up contact (Slack, 1984).

Often the potentially suicidal youth is both cognitively and emotionally fluid. The steps that are presented do not have to be followed in any sequential order, but all should be utilized. The psychological first aid outline provides a useful structure for the school staff person to be able to respond to a situation that may be unfamiliar and frightening when dealing with a youth in crisis.

SUPPORTIVE CONFRONTATION

Supportive confrontation offers a method for responding immediately by confronting the student with his or her suicidal thoughts and behaviors, making a request to stop or alter suicidal behavior and intent, and providing positive support and concern. Supportive confrontation also assumes that direct confrontation of negative, self-destructive behavior is seen by the suicidal student as being positively supportive and respectful of the person's worth.

Supportive confrontation, then, is a method of interaction that encourages positive action and prevents self-destructive behavior in an atmosphere of caring and concern. It can be accomplished through coaching a youth to a point of decision and action to not carry through with the suicidal intent, and it should be employed as early as possible. Supportive confrontation exposes thinking patterns of the youth in crisis and brings the young person to the recognition that his or her behavior is not the only alternative for resolution. To be successful, supportive confrontation must be genuine, appropriately optimistic, reality based, and consistent. There are several steps and techniques for employing supportive confrontation:

Remove accessibility to the means the person intends to use to kill themselves.

Always take a positive, affirming approach by emphasizing the person's most desirable alternatives.

Always try to sound calm and understanding.

Use constructive, specific questions to separate and define the person's problems from the confusion surrounding irrational beliefs.

Help the person understand the situation by focusing on current realities, and firmly dispute inappropriate thoughts and behaviors.

Offer direct assistance to help the youth develop a plan to address his or her helplessness or hopelessness and regain personal control.

Coach the student in a step-by-step fashion on specific actions they can use to help themselves. Affirm any level of progress, and continue until the desired level of success is achieved by the person and yourself.

Get a commitment to the initial plan and to continuing communication. Assure the person that you and other appropriate helping persons are available to listen and to help should suicidal thoughts and feelings reoccur.

Facilitate a program of follow-up and tracking of the person, including documentation of contacts and degree of progress.

Tell the person that he or she is special and unique and that you want them to live. It is important to reach any suicidal person with direct, human concern for them and their being.

Refer the student to a treatment program if more intervention is needed.

There are several things that are not done as part of supportive confrontation or other approaches with suicidal youth:

Do not disregard or trivialize observed symptomatology.

Do not respond with shock when a student expresses suicidal intent.

Do not tell the teen what they should feel or think.

Do not moralize or judge the person.

Do not be mislead by digression tactics or changing the subject to a safe topic unrelated to the suicidal behavior.

Do not dwell on the embarrassment and pain a suicide would cause family or friends of the student.

Do not try to physically remove a weapon from a suicidal person if the action will put anyone in danger.

Do not threaten disciplinary action as a means of compliance against suicidal behavior.

Do not try to solve all the problems and issues surrounding the youth; stay focused on immediate issues connected with the suicide.

Do not leave the person alone if there is any risk of self-harm.

MAKING PSYCHOLOGICAL CONTACT

To make psychological contact, one must approach the youth with a sense of confidence and concern. It is important to be accepting, non-judgmental, warm, and supportive. The primary effort is directed at allowing the youth to talk freely without showing shock or disapproval. Active listening is suggested to elicit a discussion about the suicidal youth's feelings. It is necessary to encourage the student to share ideas and feelings about why things have become troubling enough to consider suicide, and it is important to keep the youth cognitively engaged with the teacher or counselor.

Sometimes the youth is in such emotional pain that it is difficult for him or her to talk. It is important not to force the youth to interact but, instead, simply be with the person. At a time that seems right, the individual will begin to talk and share thoughts and feelings.

CLARIFYING THE PROBLEMS

It is important for the helping person to identify and specify the youth's problems but not to conduct a thorough investigation. It is important to find out what has happened, what precipitated it, when it happened, and who else may be involved. This is best accomplished by having the youth tell his or her story. The teen may very likely be confused, and the perceptions described may not reflect reality. In these instances, the helping person needs to bring focus to the discussion.

It is important to identify the precipitating event in order to identify the situation and conditions around it that caused the person to finally give in to suicidal thought.

While helping a distressed youth distinguish his or her thinking that things are hopeless from actual events, it is important for the intervening adult to act in a consistent fashion and not get caught up in the intensity of the youth's emotional distress. Realistic views and interpretations need to be gently but firmly presented to the youth.

EXAMINING POSSIBLE SOLUTIONS

Engaging the youth in an open discussion of possible solutions with the opportunity to be a part of solving his or her own problems allows the youth to regain a feeling of control. It is important as a helper not to rush into providing solutions but to allow the youth time to examine possible alternatives that can help reduce the emotional pain and the stressful event.

It is often helpful to ask about past times when the youth was feeling distressed and how he or she previously coped. If times are described when personal coping strategies were successful, it is important to point out that they may work now in the present situation.

The intervening adult must assist the youth in determining alternate solutions by describing tangible possibilities and how they might work in the situation. When helping the youth discuss alternatives, it is important to assess the positives and negatives of each of the alternatives and realistically view any obstacles to the plans. Taking time to role play can be a useful exercise in helping the youth practice the steps of a selected solution.

TAKING ACTION

It is important for the helping person to make a determination whether the current situation has lethal possibilities. If the youth does not calm down quickly and he or she has the means available to complete suicide, it is critical to not leave the youth alone but to get additional help. The next step is to arrange for the youth to be transported to the nearest hospital emergency room for stabilization and to contact the youth's family.

When the level of risk is low, there is no immediate danger to self or others, and the youth is capable of acting on his or her behalf, the helper can direct attention toward facilitating the proposed coping solutions. It is important for the helper to be clear about expectations of who is to do what. The focus is to assist the youth to be responsible for his or her own actions by working through appropriate solutions.

When it appears that a verbal contract may not be sufficient, a written agreement, called a "no suicide contract," can be established. It includes written statements that the youth will not commit or attempt suicide during a stated period of time. If, however, the youth resumes feelings of hopelessness and helplessness and begins to think of suicide, he or she agrees to contact an identified adult or suicide prevention agency. If a written contract is used, it is important to supply phone numbers, addresses, and names of staff members. Signing a contract is a mutual commitment made by the youth to access help if needed and by the helping adult to continue to offer help as needed. For those youth who do not have experience with contacting helping agencies, it is helpful to explain how services are accessed and what can be expected from them.

ESTABLISHING FOLLOW-UP CONTACT

The focus of following up is to determine if the goals of psychological first aid have been accomplished and whether the person is out of danger.

Sometimes a youth may feel embarrassed at the suicide attempt or think that he or she is crazy or weak, resulting in a sense of fear about how others may react. It is important to reassure the youth that the feelings of being out of control, experiencing the emotional pain, and having the sense of hopelessness and helplessness that accompanies suicidal intent do not mean that one is mentally ill. It is, instead, a rather human reaction to a series of unresolved, troubling problems.

The youth needs to be informed that it is important to involve others, including parents or guardians, school staff, and therapists. Although confidential issues need not be shared with everyone, certain information will need to be discussed among those who have a need to know. Follow-up contact should be clearly defined as to time and place and who is to be contacted. It is crucial to give the message to the youth that his or her life is important, that everyone associated with the person wants the youth to live, and that they will do everything possible to ensure that it happens.

A summary of what to do and what not to do in providing psychological first aid follows.

What To Do

Listen. A frank and honest discussion is the important first step toward suicide prevention. It is critical for a suicidal person to be able to talk about why he or she wants to die. Discuss his or her feelings of suicide openly and frankly. Ask questions about how she or he feels and about the reasons for those feelings.

Be honest. Admit to being frightened or uncomfortable by the suicidal thought or actions, if that is the case. Offer to try to understand the situation if the individual will describe their thoughts and feelings about it.

Access. Find out if there is a specific plan. Is there a gun at home? Where is it? Are pills collected? What are they? The more specific the plan, the more likely it is to be implemented.

Be supportive. Let the young person know the concern of the helper and the school. Break through the sense of isolation and stay close. Assure the person that suicidal impulses are temporary, and problems can be solved in spite of how bad things are now.

Take charge. Emphasize that help is at hand, and waste no time in finding it.

Get help. Do not try to handle the problem alone. Seek professional help immediately. Encourage her or him to seek help through the family physician, a suicide prevention center, a crisis intervention center, a mental health clinic, or a clergy member. If the person refuses, explain the situation to reliable family members, or call a suicide prevention center or other sources of help yourself.

Make a contract. Get a commitment, preferably in writing, that she or he will not attempt suicide.

Vital Questions

Have your problems been getting you down so much lately that you've been thinking of harming yourself?

How would you harm yourself?

Do you have the means available?

Have you ever attempted suicide?

What has been keeping you alive so far?

What is your hurry? Why do it now?

What do you think the odds are that you will kill yourself?

What do you think that the future holds in store for you?

What Not to Do

Do not assume the situation will cure itself.

Do not leave the person alone if the situation is lethal.

Do not act shocked at what the suicidal person tells you.

Do not challenge or dare the person to commit suicide.

Do not argue or debate moral issues with the suicidal person.

Do not be sworn to secrecy about the suicide attempt.

ASSESSING LEVEL OF INTERVENTION NEEDED

Throughout the process of providing psychological first aid, the teacher or staff person making contact with the troubled youth needs to be assessing the degree of risk presented.

It is recognized that the teacher or staff person's ability to assess the level of danger is limited by the available information about the youth's crisis state.

Once it is suspected that the youth is potentially suicidal, it is best to quickly approach the individual in a caring, nonjudgmental manner about their intent and reasons for it. The query can begin with a question such as, "You haven't seemed like your old self lately. Have your problems been getting you down so much recently that you've been thinking about harming yourself?"

When genuinely and supportively confronted about their suicidal feelings and thoughts, most youths will answer honestly. An initial problem is that some adults seem hesitant to bring up the subject of suicide for fear that they will be planting the idea in the mind of a youth who had not thought of it before. Suicide in youth is not spontaneous behavior, and mentioning the word will not cause a nonsuicidal youth to go out and kill themselves. If, however, the student has been engaged in the process of suicidal ideation, then inquiring about his or her feelings and intentions might very well lead the youth to believe that someone finally understands and may greatly relieve the immediate danger of the crisis event.

If the person admits to being suicidal, it is imperative that the degree of risk is assessed as soon as possible. Always begin the assessment by asking the five specific questions described under psychological first aid to determine the nature of suicidal intent and the specific plan.

Next, it is important to determine the lethal possibilities of the proposed method. How quickly could the youth die if they do what they plan to do? Is the intent to take some sleeping pills or slash their wrists?

Is the youth planning to shoot themselves in the head as soon as they get home or get drunk and take a few pills? The higher the level of lethality in the plan, the greater is the degree of risk.

The proximity of helping resources is critical to determine. How close is the youth physically and geographically to others who could aid in rescue if necessary? Does the youth plan to leave a note? To whom is it addressed? Will information given in the suicide note direct a rescue attempt away from the suicidal individual? Are there other people nearby who care about the youth, such as relatives, friends, or neighbors? In general, the greater the distance the youth is from those who could rescue him or her in an emergency, the greater is the degree of risk. It is important to note that many youth's suicides occur at or near the youth's home or school. They most often occur at a time, however, when the youth assumes no one is around to stop the attempt.

The next question that must be asked of the youth is, "Have you ever tried to kill yourself in the past?" Usually the strongest behavioral warning is a previously attempted suicide. If, during the assessment, the youth indicates that he or she has previously attempted suicide, the following factors are helpful in further determining the degree of risk.

How dangerous was the previous attempt? Did the youth ingest five aspirins or 75 barbiturate tablets when the attempt was made? The greater the danger potential of the attempt, the higher is the current risk.

What was the youth's impression of the level of danger? Even if what the youth did during the previous attempt was not dangerous, it still could indicate higher current risk if the youth had the impression that it had lethal potential. If a suicidal youth learned that five pills did not have lethal effect the first time, they may try to swallow 100 tablets or more in the next attempt.

Did the youth participate in rescuing themselves during the past event? What were the chances of someone else intervening to prevent the suicide? After they took the pills, did they tell someone what they had done? Did they drive themselves to the hospital? Did they place themselves in a position where they could be rescued? If the chances were good that they would be rescued or if they assisted in their own rescue by any means, the present risk may be somewhat lower.

How long ago did the most recent attempt occur? Was it three or four years ago or a few weeks ago? Generally, the more recent the attempt, particularly if made within the past six months, the higher is the current risk.

The more risk indicators present, the higher is the likelihood of a suicide attempt. A summary of the criteria is a specific plan, availability of method, location, time, ingestion of alcohol or drugs, inaccessible for rescue, lack of support (friends, family), loss, previous attempts, and chronic physical or emotional problems including depression (Deaton & Morgan, 1992, p. 28).

DEPRESSION IN YOUTH SUICIDE

Because elements of clinical depression are evident in over half the cases of completed youth suicide, it is important to assess the degree of depression the youth seems to be exhibiting (Sargent, 1989). Depression should not be confused with the temporary feelings of unhappiness that everyone experiences over specific situations. In contrast, children and youth suffering from serious depressive disorders have not felt good for months or years. Emotional conditions affect feelings, thoughts, and behaviors. Like others in any age group, depressed adolescents can experience feelings of lack of self-worth, emptiness, anxiety, loneliness, helplessness, and hopelessness.

The following questions will assist in further assessing the need for intervention: "Have you had sad, anxious, or empty feelings for a long time?" "Are you feeling tired all the time?" "Have you seemed to have lost interest or pleasure in activities that you formerly enjoyed?" "Are you having trouble sleeping or do you find yourself sleeping all the time?" "Have you experienced recent appetite or weight changes?" "Do you have feelings of worthlessness, helplessness, or hopelessness?" "Have you been experiencing difficulty in concentrating, remembering, and making decisions?" Positive answers to four or more of the questions indicate a higher degree of risk. In addition, youth will sometimes tend to act out their depression through aggressive behavior, running away, or becoming delinquent. A youth who is experiencing several symptoms of depression for longer than a few weeks or who is recently doing poorly in school; seems socially withdrawn, uncaring, or overly impulsive; and is no longer interested in activities once enjoyed should be considered at higher risk.

Once the degree of risk has been assessed, it is helpful to determine the level of appropriate intervention. Three levels of intervention with corresponding actions applicable to the school setting are suggested. There are moderate, high, and extreme risk levels (Deaton & Morgan, 1990).

A youth determined to be at *moderate* risk could engage in a suicide attempt but does not have a plan or strong motivation for execution. Some level of support is available, and some internal controls and coping skills are present. The student is willing to talk with others about alternatives to suicide.

A student at *high* risk for suicide is someone who has made a tangible plan and likely will carry out a suicide attempt without some kind of intervention. Initial assessment indicates that the plan and the means of potential suicide would definitely be lethal and that there is a strong probability that the youth may not be able to use self-control measures to avoid suicidal behavior.

The *extreme* risk youth requires immediate intervention to ensure physical survival. The youth will likely have made a previous attempt and will act on their plan if there is no monitoring and control by someone.

Steps to be taken at each level are described:

Moderate Risk Suicide Attempter
Express concern and explore the thoughts and feelings of the student. Explain that information shared by the student cannot remain confidential if a suicide attempt appears likely.
Determine how much the parents know about the student's feelings about suicide. Notify parents if they are not already aware, unless there is a compelling reason why parental notification will present a greater hazard to the student.
Refer the student to a school counselor or psychologist if indicated.
Provide the student with a list of mental health professionals in the community.
Provide weekly contact and support.
Inform school staff who are in daily contact with the student about the risk and request that they provide regular monitoring and support.
Consider the use of short-term counseling or peer group support at the school.

High Risk Suicide Attempter
Refer the student to a school counselor and notify the principal immediately.
The counselor will meet with the student and assess the seriousness of the attempt.
The means and plan of the suicide attempt should be evaluated, and if needed, an intervention plan is developed.
If present, such items as pills, poison, or firearms are to be removed if it can be done safely.
Contact the parent or guardian and inform them of the school's efforts.
Determine whether the student is receiving counseling and if the therapist is aware of and treating the student's suicide issues. If not, suggest appropriate treatment resources.
Monitor the behavior and mood of the student throughout the day.

Extreme Risk Suicide Attempter
The student must not be left alone.
Parents or guardian must be notified immediately and requested to come to
    school.
The staff member involved with the student and principal will meet with the
    parent to discuss the situation and develop a plan.
The student can leave the school only with a parent or mental health
    professional.
The staff member will follow up the next day with the student.
Teacher and other staff members regularly involved with the student will be
    informed of the outcome.
The school will collaborate with the primary treatment agency or therapist of
    the suicidal youth.

ENGAGING PARENTS AND PEERS

Parents

Parents must be contacted as soon as possible whenever a child has
been identified as being at risk. The parents have a legal and ethical right
to know such information, and teachers and staff personnel are mandated
to inform the parent or legal guardian when the youth is determined to be
at risk to themselves or others. Contact with the parent should be made
by the designated staff member in the intervention plan for the student.

The information may come as a shock to the parents if the youth has
not presented suicidal feelings and at-risk behaviors at home or if the
parents have been interpreting the symptoms as being of little concern
(Figley, 1988, pp. 83–109).

Experience shows that when information is shared in a sensitive and
caring fashion, with parents being supported and encouraged to become
part of the intervention process, the shock and trauma can be greatly
lessened. When parents are receptive and willing to collaborate in the
intervention effort, the following guidelines are helpful to give parents
guidance and direction:

Advise parents of the level of risk and the actions of the school to assist the
    youth, parents, and therapist, if appropriate.
Tell the parents to consult a physician who can determine the possibility of
    physical causes of the behavior and feelings of the child or adolescent, and
    make appropriate referral to mental health professionals.
Urge the parents to immediately contact a suicide prevention center if the youth
    appears likely to make a suicidal attempt.

Encourage the parents to communicate care and support to the troubled youth.

Encourage the parents to talk honestly and openly with the child instead of avoiding the subject because of their own feelings.

Advise the parents to reassure their child that expressing his or her own feelings and fears will not result in rejection by the family.

Provide the parents with basic information on identifying the warning signs and symptomatology of suicide.

Advise the parents to observe their child for continuing behavior and to report all at-risk behavior observations to the attending physician, therapist, school counselor, or other contact person.

Strongly urge the parent to follow up with identified therapists and school personnel so that the intervention effort can continue toward resolution.

Encourage the parent to consider modifying their activities and schedule to accommodate needs of their child.

Tell the parent to not leave the youth alone if he or she becomes suicidal. The parents should then immediately call the local suicide prevention center for further direction or take the youth directly to the emergency room of a hospital.

Assure the parents that it is appropriate to be hopeful and to express hope to their child.

Dealing with Parental Reluctance and Resistance

Sometimes parents are reluctant and may outright deny serious suicidal behavior in their children. They may be simply overwhelmed by an array of family problems that does not allow room to accommodate one more serious situation. Some families find the possibility of suicide to be so foreign to their values that they are compelled to deny any possibility that it could exist in their inner circle. Professionals recognize that it is a healthy defense for the family to initially deny such negative, extreme possibilities as child suicide with one of their members. It is also natural for the family to try and solve serious problems of one of their members without outside intervention. However, there are ways to understand and work successfully with the family.

Denial of the Problem

Possibly the most common negative initial reaction of parents, denial of the problem, is often only a first reaction that can change as the shock of first hearing the information is over. Relating the factual information gained from the assessment with the child and using direct language about the circumstances and intent of the student will often break through denial. In only a very few cases is it impossible to get the parents' compliance and cooperation to work with the school or other agencies on behalf of the child. In such situations where there is extreme suicide risk, it is necessary to act without the parents' assistance to insure the safety of the student.

Guilt

Parents are likely to feel a great sense of guilt upon hearing that a child is suicidal. Our society places an extreme sense of responsibility on the family for the outcome of their children's behavior, successes, and failures. Children are viewed as a reflection of the parents' concern or lack of it. The school representative communicates realistic hope and describes the limitations of the parents' responsibility and the limits of the control they have over behaviors and feelings of their child. The parental relationship with the youth may need to be examined, and parents may need to be encouraged to share their feelings openly with the youth.

Fear

The feeling associated with losing control over a situation creates fear in parents. Sometimes, when they hear "treatment" or "intervention plan," the parents' fears may cause them to withdraw from the discussion or react by trying to control the planning decisions. The key to working through parental resistance is to try to understand the source and motivation of the fear. Once the parents' point of view is clear, it may be possible to assure them that they will share in all intervention decisions and that they are still in control as the parents.

Admitting and Sharing Vulnerability

Most parents do not want school officials to see that they are not perfect. They may be even less likely to want others to know that they have a family member troubled enough to consider suicide. In addition to empathy and understanding, it can be gently pointed out that the school is already involved and knows about the situation. The school will make efforts to handle the matter in confidence as far as possible. It is also helpful to ask the parents to think of ways that the school or other professionals in the community might be helpful to them about the problem.

Frustration and Anger

Some parents will react with frustration and anger at hearing that the school feels their child is suicidal. It is important to understand that these feelings often come from the loss of hope that things will get better magically by themselves. Frustration and anger by family members can be misinterpreted by the listener as absolute resistance rather than as an opportunity to clarify the source of the feelings. The key is to help the angry parent in pinpointing the feelings and their source. Advise the parent that it is all right to have such feelings, because they are human and natural responses and reflect genuine concern. Discuss constructive actions with the parents, and try to channel the energy toward focusing on what the parents can do to help themselves and their child through the situation. If successful, the effort may open up entirely new lines of communication between the child, the parents, and the school.

Depression and Despair

Sometimes youth who are clinically depressed became the way they are partially because they grew up with a depressed parent. If the parent is also depressed or hopeless, it is important to focus on helping the depressed parent before they can be expected to help their troubled child. It is usually advisable to encourage the parent to keep life and routines as normal as possible and to develop a support system to bolster them during the crisis with the child. If indicated, encourage the parent to seek professional help for themselves and to deal with other related family problems.

Peers

Most often, a peer is the first person to hear or observe another student experiencing suicidal ideation. One of the best methods of suicide prevention for a school to undertake is to make training available to the student population about the signs and symptoms of suicide and what to do if another student talks about killing themselves. Research on the outcome of training students in understanding the dynamics and early detection of adolescent suicide has shown that the training does not reduce the incidence of suicide attempts in the student population. The prevention curriculum is a more promising place to reduce or prevent suicide and other destructive acts in students. However, training older children and adolescents in understanding how to recognize signs of suicidal intent and knowing what direct action to take is an important part of the prevention and intervention plan of the school because it provides an essential avenue for early detection (Shaffer et al., 1990, pp. 3152–55; Tierney et al., 1991, pp. 88–89).

Training topics on the dynamics and signs of suicidal thought and intent can be developed from the material described earlier in this chapter. The Wisconsin publication *A Guide to Curriculum Planning in Suicide Prevention* (1990) details plans on training topics and outlines for students.

In addition to providing factual information, it can be helpful to suggest techniques in peer communications and referral of troubled adolescents when intervention is indicated.

Being Available to Talk about It

Peers should be willing to talk with another student who wants to talk about feelings of suicide or hopelessness. A discussion will not encourage the person to become more suicidal; on the contrary, it will help them to know that someone is willing to be a friend. Do not try to turn the discussion off or immediately offer advice by saying such things as "Think about how much better off you are than most people." Such comments only make the suicidal person feel more hopeless than before.

Being a Good Listener

What the suicidal person may need is a peer to listen to them. Being willing to listen will show the person some concern and that they are not being judged for having hopeless or self-destructive feelings.

Sharing Feelings

Peers can briefly share their own experiences and similar feelings if they have been through something like the suicidal student. An example could be, "I think I can appreciate how you are feeling. I remember how awful it was for me to break up with Tim last year. I cried for a long time and couldn't do anything." Sharing a similarly felt experience should be kept brief, however. The focus is on the feelings of the troubled person, not the listener.

Being Honest

Ask whether a method of suicide has been considered, whether any specific plans have been made, and if any steps have been taken toward carrying it out. If he or she says they have, concern should be expressed for them. Say directly, "I want you to live." These words, said genuinely and with care and concern, can reach through and be the connection to save a life. If frightened by the person's suicidal expressions, it is appropriate to be honest and say so. Honest reactions will convey genuine concern, more than faked expressions of calm.

Getting Help

Whenever it appears that a troubled peer might be suicidal or destructive to themselves or others, other help must be secured. Sometimes the person who confides in a peer will try and make that person promise to keep it a secret. This is a secret that cries to be told, and if the secret is kept, a friend may be lost. Perhaps the student can think of a helpful person he or she would talk to. Ask the person about key people in their lives, such as teachers, coaches, school counselors, family members, or other respected adults. If the suicidal person will not talk to one of them, act immediately and get help. The listening student must then go to the appropriate resource at the school. The student has turned to a peer for help, but sometimes the help cannot be delivered by a friend alone.

Using Help If Suicide Happens

In spite of all efforts, there may be a suicide or other violent death at the school. Such tragic events affect everyone in the school, faculty as well as students. Most people will feel a surge of different emotions. Often there is shock because no one expected that a young person would die. There can be sadness and anger because the act has made everyone uncomfortable and aware of the reality of death as a possibility with those close to them.

The services provided by the school described in Chapter 8 help students deal with shock and grief and better understand death situations.

REFERRAL

Once discovered as suicidal, the adolescent at risk must be referred for professional assessment and treatment. The safety of the youth is the most important consideration for any decisions in the intervention plan. Problems of some individuals may be too volatile to be handled within the school setting. In those cases, referral to therapists in private practice or adolescent treatment agencies that accept depressed and suicidal adolescents should be made. There may be other longstanding problems that underlie a youth's depression and suicidal behavior that require extensive professional intervention with the youth and the family. The time, expertise, and energy necessary for extended intervention are most often too much for treatment resources in the school setting to be expected to provide.

Referral commonly begins with parents or school authorities sending an adolescent to a professional when they detect a clustering of depressive symptoms, acting out behaviors, or suicidal threats. In the school setting, an internal referral to a guidance counselor or school psychologist might be made when a teacher notices that the student appears to be losing interest in school activities or has become sad and lethargic. The parent, as well, may seek out intervention for the child at a community mental health center in response to the youth's use of drugs or alcohol and presentation of vague suicidal threats.

Resources

Community resources, agencies, and private practitioners need to be evaluated to ensure the competencies of those to whom students at risk may be sent. At a time of crisis, the staff who meet with parents need to know which services are appropriate and available. Questions about effective sources of referral include: What is the exact nature of services provided? What are the costs and policies for acceptance of private insurance and medical clients? What is the availability of services? Are clients seen after business hours? Is there a waiting list? Will the professional or service agency accept troubled adolescents who are not already clients? Does the professional or helping agency specialize in treating adolescents with suicidal intent? Who are the contact persons, and what are the telephone numbers and locations of the offices?

Schools should contact local professionals and visit the major service agencies to review programs and develop protocols for referral and follow-up. It is important to verify whether agencies and those in private practice actually deliver the services offered in a timely, effective way.

Because many suicides involve alcohol or other drugs and elements of depression, identified resources must be available to provide assessment and treatment in these areas as well.

A novel approach for developing a comprehensive list of available services in a community is to utilize students themselves. They can conduct the community survey of resources to establish a network of those professionals and agencies identified for referral purposes. In addition, students might better understand the range of helping services and develop the idea of receiving help when in crisis. When the community as a whole is perceived by teenagers as being engaged in showing concern for youth as well as the quality of its services and resources, students' and general public awareness increases and stigma is reduced.

Referral Decisions

The decision to decide to offer supportive counseling within the school setting versus referring to specialized, outside resources begins with a careful assessment of the student's needs. For the youth who is considered a low risk for suicide, counseling can be provided within the school environment. Explain the reasons for counseling and identify the concerns, issues, and goals that will require work. Be direct with the youth about information that will be shared with parents, guardians, or others who may have a need to know.

For the suicidal student who fits into the moderate or higher risk categories, discuss with them the need for professional help outside the school setting. Share with the youth that the matter is extremely serious and that they need a type of therapy that the school will not be able to provide. Involving the youth in planning and explaining the need for specialized services will greatly improve the chances of a successful referral.

Prepare the Youth and Family for the Referral

Tell the youth as concretely as possible what to expect in the referral, intake, and treatment process and where services will be offered. Explain the kinds of programs offered and the treatment approaches of the referral agency or therapist.

If there will be a waiting period, explain available interim help by the school or others.

Anticipate any resistance or obstacles, such as lack of transportation or costs to the family for services. Go over all the steps from initially seeking help to meeting with the therapist.

Explain how the school and the referral agency will be sharing information and coordinating their helping efforts together.

Reassure the youth and family that they made a good decision to share problems and concerns with the school about the potential suicide and that they are taking the right step to follow through with the referral.

Follow up with the youth and the referral agency or therapist to be sure that contact was made and appointments were kept.

Prepare the Referral Source for the Youth

Contact the referral source to: confirm all basic requirements, such as time, place, and availability of services; and go over information pertaining to the suicidal youth's situation. Give the reasons why the school is making the referral, including a description of all observed and reported suicidal behaviors, verbal threats, and current situational cues that may be present. Share the key assessment item information, including level of imminent risk, lethality and intent, predisposing factors and precipitating events, level of depression, level of compliance of the youth, and identified coping skills and resources of the youth and family. Describe how the school became aware of the youth's suicide potential. Ask the referral source if the school can provide other assistance. Finally, discuss collaboration and contact between the referral source and the school.

Monitor the Student's Activities

Check with the youth daily until the student has connected with the referral source. Continue to support the youth and positively reinforce the decision to seek help. Contact the youth and parent to assess progress and the extent and severity of risk. Share pertinent information about school behavior and progress with the referral service.

Determine the Level and Degree of Follow-up Needed

Let the treatment agency or therapist know the policy and follow-up procedures established by the school. Ask what the school can do, and maintain a log of contacts with the treatment specialist, the parents, and the youth. Request a summary report of the therapist's view of progress and a termination report upon completion of treatment.

REENTRY ACTIVITIES: THE SCHOOL'S ROLE

The complexity of life issues and feelings of hopelessness and helplessness that led a student to attempt suicide do not go away when the problem is identified and a referral is made for outside assistance. The student who has attempted suicide often is at greater risk for suicide during the next few weeks and months. It is extremely important to closely monitor the reentry into school and to maintain close contact with parents and mental health professionals working with the student.

Reentry into School

It can be difficult for a troubled student to come back to school. They are aware that the parents were called by the school, some teachers and staff are aware of what occurred, and a plan of intervention and monitoring has been devised. It will be even more awkward if the student has made an actual attempt and it is generally known around the school.

A counselor or crisis response team member must be assigned to coordinate support for the student and maintain contact between the parents, the outside treatment provider, teachers as appropriate, and other school staff. The contact person is allowed some flexibility to be able to respond quickly if additional crisis occurs with the student. The student's classroom teachers need to be informed that the youth is at risk and be encouraged to both observe for continuing signs of instability and to provide support to the youth. Academic expectations in general should remain the same for the youth as for others in the class. Establishing consistency and stability in daily expectations and structure in school is important.

If the student will be absent from school for several weeks after a suicide attempt because of hospitalization in a treatment facility, the school should follow several steps while the student is away from the school setting (Deaton & Morgan, 1992).

Obtain a written release of information form signed by the parents that makes it possible for confidential treatment information to be shared between school personnel and treatment providers.

Inform the student's teachers regarding the number of probable days of absence.

Instruct teachers to provide the student with assignments to be completed while away, if appropriate.

Maintain contact with the student to keep them informed of school events of interest.

Seek recommendations for aftercare at the school from the student's therapist. A counselor or crisis response team member should attend the discharge meeting at the hospital.

The counselor or crisis response team member should convey information to appropriate school staff regarding the aftercare plan.

Once a student returns to school, a counselor or crisis response team member should maintain regular contact with the individual.

The school should maintain contact with the parents, providing information about the student's progress and informing them of any changes in the treatment plan.

At-Risk Student Monitoring

All students who have been identified as being at any level of risk of or who have attempted suicide need to be closely observed upon returning to school. The purpose of monitoring is: to observe any changes in the student's behavior that may signal increasing or lessening of risk and report it to the appropriate response team member and/or counselor; to identify and correct situations where the school may be contributing negatively to readjustment; to actively engage in opportunities for the teacher and staff to offer support to the student; to maintain daily or regular contact with the students, teachers, or other staff in regular contact with the student; and to have daily contact with the student at risk, taking care that the level of monitoring does not cause a student to feel embarrassed.

Additional Support Activities

Support Group

A school-supported peer group led by a trained group leader can provide support and mutual self-help for students who have been at risk for suicide. The group does not take the place of counseling provided by the school or by outside professionals. Troubled students meeting together with adult guidance to discuss school-related problems and strategies to alleviate them often meet one or two times a week in a guided self-help format.

Peer Support

Fellow students of the at-risk youth who has attempted suicide and returned to school need to be aware that sometimes it can be difficult for them as well as for the returning student. When living sometimes seems harder than dying, facing acquaintances and friends again may seem the hardest of all. If the at-risk youth is a close friend, it is important to understand that they may experience feelings of being uncomfortable and unsure of what to say or do and may avoid the person. Peers can be encouraged to say to the at-risk student how they felt when they heard about the suicide attempt and how they so much wanted their friend to live. The connection with peers and the sense of being cared for can often be the glue that helps put things together for the troubled youth.

In summary, the reasons students choose to engage in at-risk behaviors, including attempting to kill themselves, are varied and complex. The school can greatly reduce the risk of suicide by providing reentry programs, monitoring efforts, and additional support activities with the student and their parents. Even though the school cannot be expected to eliminate all the possibilities of suicide among its students, it can provide a comprehensive, caring response in concert with the family and other community agencies.

6

Postvention

All of the activities that are planned in advance and conducted in response to the death of a school member are considered postvention. The primary purpose is to assist students and staff with their immediate reactions of grief, shock, and loss. Other important reasons include providing a caring response by the school and assisting individuals and groups with forming some immediate closure and moving ahead.

The major responses in postvention include grief and support counseling, discussions about the death in classes and other activities, debriefing sessions for groups of students and staff who were associated with the deceased, identifying those who will need further individual help, and involvement with memorial services. For some situations, postvention responses to grief and loss by students may be needed beyond a few days or weeks following the event.

Developing a school plan for postvention response is critically important in order to have activities and services available when needed, to be able to maintain control over the situation, and to deal with the incident in a reasonable time frame. The authors have responded to requests of several schools following a death in which no prior plan for handling similar incidents was in place. We found that administrators and counselors spent many hours trying to find and secure assistance from mental health professionals in the community, seeking to cover a deluge of requests for information, and attempting to handle misinformation about the incident. At the same time, they had to deal with immediate needs of saddened and upset students as well as maintain some level of regular, daily activities of the school. School staff had to attempt to manage the multiple pressures of the immediate situation while they became overburdened and fatigued themselves.

In one school, a junior high girl committed suicide, and the principal learned about it late in the afternoon. He decided not to tell the students because the news of the suicide of a classmate might upset them. Several students learned of the death on the way to school the next morning, became very upset, and went to school, where they immediately spread the news. Most students reacted strongly, and school staff felt unprepared to help. Because of the upset and confusion, the school did not return to its normal schedule for several days. In another situation, a rural school district did have a minimal plan and had provided some teacher training in youth suicide. However, their resources were overwhelmed when a high school student committed suicide and a teacher who had been terminally ill died of cancer on the same day. Fortunately, prior training included ways to access outside postvention specialists who could assist with developing a specific response plan and provide direct services.

Our experience consistently is that school administrators will spend much more time dealing with unplanned situations than they will in investing in a plan and taking necessary steps to put it in place. It is human nature to believe that an unexpected fatality or series of deaths, particularly suicides and homicides, will never happen at "our" school or community. It is also natural to treat death situations at the school or other workplaces as a taboo subject that one does not discuss openly or in advance of its unlikely occurrence.

The concept of postvention is that immediate, planned responses to shock, upset, grief, and loss that individuals and groups experience can greatly assist them to deal with the loss and to return to normal daily routines quickly. Postvention also provides a closure ceremony or structured process for people involved in the same incident or loss, wherein they individually and collectively express their feelings and thoughts of loss and grief and then move on to what they usually do at work and school. The process has been called the modern version of the wake.

DEVELOPING A POSTVENTION PLAN

Some schools develop district-wide plans, while in others, each building will have its own. Many state departments of education have established detailed guidelines and resource materials to assist local districts with planning and program information (see Appendix B for examples).

A planning committee usually consists of school counselors, psychologists, social workers, teachers, administrators, and a librarian. Student representatives should definitely be members, although they have apparently not been widely used. Some schools use outside consultants or community professionals with specialized experience in the field to assist in planning and training staff in postvention procedures.

Planning for postvention response concerns several key questions: What criteria will apply to determine if an incident requires a major response effort? What activities will the school be prepared for and choose to offer? What services will be offered to staff, to students, and to all school members? Who will perform the services? What services will be provided to those individuals or groups who require further help in getting over the current incident? What community resources are present to assist with the array of services that might be needed?

DETERMINING THE NEED FOR POSTVENTION RESPONSE

Not every situation requires an organized postvention response, and it depends upon whether the incident overwhelms the ability of a group of people in the school setting to handle and get over the incident with their own personal resources. For instance, the infrequent occurrence of an accidental death of a school member, although troubling and saddening, will often be handled by the school community without special postvention activities except for some individuals who are especially affected.

Several deaths in quick succession will overburden the ability of individuals or whole groups to cope. In one school, two people died the same evening in separate occurrences. Distraught school officials said that they could cope with either death had they been some time apart, and considerable postvention effort was required for students and staff.

Certain kinds of fatalities almost always signal the need for an organized response. A student suicide, multiple fatalities or serious injuries, younger rather than older victims, and previous attempts to help the deceased person get through life-threatening illness, injury, or suicide are situations almost always requiring planned responses.

The meaning attached to the death or other threatening incident to those at the school is the most important indicator of the need for postvention and may be more important than the factual severity of the occurrence. In one rural school located on an interstate, there was an accident involving two school buses when students were boarding the bus on the way to school. Although there were no serious injuries, the accident occurred in dense fog common to the area. Parents and school staff had often worried that such an accident might occur and that several children would be killed. When the accident finally did become reality, the adults were anxious and overwhelmed to the extent that a group debriefing was required for teachers, bus drivers, and other staff.

Having a comprehensive plan in place is most important because it is not possible to anticipate emergencies or tragedies or the needs of those involved. Therefore, planning for major occurrences and having people in the school and community designated to assist in specific roles when needed become most important.

The authors have observed that having some plan in place helps people at the school visualize and anticipate the sorts of things that could conceivably happen together with appropriate and practical responses. We have seen that in those situations with no prior planning or anticipation, those in charge could not overcome their own shock and disbelief or imagine the needs of those affected by the incident or the kinds of responses needed to assist them.

ACUTE AND LONG-TERM STRESS RESPONSES

The acute stress response is the focus of postvention concerns. It is defined as the immediate reaction to the loss and shock of the incident. It was first described and treated by emergency services responders (Mitchell, 1983), who found that personnel responding to disasters and multiple casualty incidents could get over the incident more quickly and with a sense of resolution with short-term, immediate interventions like those suggested now in school postvention activities. Further, those who do not have the opportunity to express and deal with their feelings and thoughts about a severe incident often will have the stress of several unresolved incidents accumulate in a pattern of chronic stress.

Treatment strategies for acute stress responses differ from both long-term, chronic stress and posttraumatic stress disorder (PTSD). Chronic stress is the wear and tear on a person from the long-term effects of a variety of life stresses. Although the stressors may include the death of someone close, they typically also include pressures from work, financial, health, divorce, and other sources. The treatment for long-term stress includes accurately assessing the sources and developing stress management strategies to alleviate the pressures from them. Stress management techniques include those things that the person can change, such as time management, altering one's reaction to the stress (such as learning to deal with an unfriendly supervisor), and improving mental and physical health in order to become more resistant to the effects of stress (Mitchell & Bray, 1990, pp. 99–127).

PTSD is described as the reaction and response to a traumatic event that is beyond the usual experience and coping ability of the individual (Leenaars & Wenckstern, 1991, pp. 174–75). The *Diagnostic and Statistical Manual of Mental Disorders* (DSM-III, revised, 1987), published by the American Psychiatric Association, has a detailed description of the condition and its usual symptoms. However, we agree with Leenaars and Wenckstern (1991, p. 175) that a distinction is required between disorder and response when referring to posttrauma. Disorders require detailed diagnostic and treatment procedures by specialist professionals. Acute stress reactions (responses) by those who are otherwise psychologically normal need only brief intervention.

The Everstines, psychologists specializing in PTSD treatment and clinical research (Everstine et al., 1993), distinguish between trauma and stress responses. They strongly believe that "trauma" is the more precise term because it describes typical reactions of people to deeply unsettling events that cause not only stress but also loss, grieving, or shock in varying combinations.

We prefer the term "acute stress response" to "posttraumatic disorder" when referring to postvention activities. "Acute stress" refers to the period during the first hours and days following the loss or incident. "Posttraumatic disorder" includes both the acute phase and later difficulties often experienced by adults who were child sexual abuse victims or former combat veterans.

A key difference between immediate acute stress and long-term PTSD lies in the response activities and treatment indicated for individuals and groups affected by the trauma. Generally, in acute stress activities, the focus is on having individuals go through the incident factually and realistically and express their current feelings and thoughts about the deceased and the incident. In long-term PTSD disorders, affected individuals find it too painful to relive the total experience, particularly in one or a few counseling sessions. Also, they typically have repressed much of the actual event and will be able to recall details only over a long period of time in counseling sessions involving much support, interpretation, and reconstruction of the event through professional therapy (Mitchell & Bray, 1990, pp. 29–34).

Perhaps the only procedure common to PTSD and acute stress is group support by those individuals who have been involved in a common experience. In long-term PTSD, groups are made up of people who have shared a common type of experience, such as women who were sexually abused as children. In acute stress postvention groups, the members not only experienced the same type of trauma but also were part of the same event.

It is also true that people with either acute stress or PTSD who have experienced the same or similar events will be affected differently and react dissimilarly. Such factors as prior life experiences, moral values, personal support systems, and previous and current stress all combine in various ways to make up the unique reactions of individuals affected by significant stresses.

Postvention experts in several fields, including emergency medical and fire service (Mitchell, 1983), schools (Leenaars & Wenckstern, 1991), and the general child and adult populations (Everstine & Everstine, 1993) all strongly suggest the same set of procedures and activities for postvention assistance for those affected by a traumatic incident. Because there has been little comparative long-term research on the usefulness of postvention, the agreement from practical experience of those in widely disparate fields provides important validation to current practice.

DETERMINING POSTVENTION ACTIONS OF THE SCHOOL

Although every situation will vary in terms of services needed, schools will need to plan in advance for what they will agree to offer in their postvention responses. All plans call for providing some form of drop-in counseling services for students, but there is wide variance in choosing to host or participate in memorial services.

Local values and available services in the community are figured into decisions about who will be designated to perform needed services.

The Overall Postvention Plan

Schools will vary in the details of their own plan, depending upon such factors as school district policy, staff resources, rural/urban differences, religious groups in the community, and recent death occurrences.

Practices by schools around the country and the authors' experiences have led to a list of common policies and responses that are indicated.

Postvention Plan and Practices

Develop a comprehensive plan complete with procedures, activities, and designated responsible persons.

Designate the spokesperson to the media about the incident.

Determine who will be the central person to direct and decide upon the school's response to death situations requiring organized postvention.

There must be initial planning following any incident to address the reaction and need for services that considers: the reactions of staff, students, and other community members to the incident; the kinds of activities that will need to be provided; whether an outside postvention specialist will be required for consultation in planning; and available personnel both within the school and from the community who will be needed.

Notify staff and students of the incident factually and clearly.

Follow the regular school class and activity schedule to the extent possible.

Initiate the "empty desk" procedure the day following if the incident is a student death. This activity involves a staff member following the deceased student's regular schedule of classes and activities the day following the death and is described in this chapter.

Select and staff drop-in counseling rooms for the day of and day after the incident.

Provide a group debriefing session for close associates of the deceased.

Determine the needs of staff, and select appropriate postvention services if needed.

Identify any individuals who may need follow-up assistance.

Consider whether to participate in memorial services initiated outside the school by family members or close associates of the deceased.

Identify and schedule training and educational needs for students and staff.

Schools vary considerably in their focus and selection of activities for their overall plans. The perceived mandate by the community and their professional values as educators combined with the reality of available resources will often govern the focus of organized efforts. Some developing case law on the schools' responsibility in student suicide has moved toward requiring that a response plan be in place.

Developing the Planning Committee

It has been found useful in our experience to involve representatives from community agencies, parent groups, and students as well as school administrators, counselors, social workers, and teachers in developing the school plan. If planning input is limited to only school professionals, the community, parents, and students will not feel personally invested in the effort. Also, the school will miss the opportunity to learn about the needs and the ways that people like to receive help in postvention efforts.

Contingency Planning for Emergencies

A Murphy's Law in emergency services is that no actual incident will exactly match the one described in the plan and that the situation will occur at the time least convenient for those who have to respond to it. Having a plan in place provides the tools for those who must creatively plan within a short time frame for the death incident. They will also know what the school has determined in advance to be their responsibility. Finally, those in charge of the postvention response will have at their disposal a list of resources both within and outside the school.

Communications about the Incident and Leadership

Designating one person to be the spokesperson to the media and others outside the school helps keep information clear and reduces the tendency for several different versions of what happened to develop. It also frees time for others with active roles in the postvention process to focus on their tasks with fewer interruptions.

One individual is designated to be in charge of the school's postvention plan. Consideration should be given to who would be best suited to direct each incident as it occurs. It will usually be too burdensome to have the same person each time. A staff member who was very close to the deceased or their family and close associates should not have to be in charge of postvention activities. A single designated person may not be available when needed on short notice because of sickness, travel, or other reasons. In some schools it is assumed that the principal or other administrator should automatically be in charge of postvention events, but some school officials are comfortable and competent with doing so while others are not. Therefore, planning should take into account the need for several people who are trained in critical incident stress, the school's postvention plan, and who are likely to be available when the need occurs.

Initial Planning and Response

Although each incident will vary in circumstance and although a death situation rarely can be predicted, there are several basic planning considerations for all cases.

Reactions of Staff, Students, and Other Community Members

Although some feeling of shock, loss, and mourning will be expressed in every incident by those who knew the deceased, their exact reactions will vary.

The most important factor will be how closely associated people felt to the victim. Teachers, counselors, and coaches who worked more intensively and invested themselves in the deceased will be more affected than others. The close friends of the victim are, of course, most deeply touched. Those staff and close friends often will require individual and group efforts targeted specifically to their needs.

How closely related to the school the victim was at the time of death is an important factor in the intensity of reaction. When the death occurs during Christmas or summer vacation, it is felt differently by the school community than if it had occurred during the school term. Two suicides occurred within a few months of each other in a rural high school. One student had dropped out of school weeks before she took her life. The student and school had started to become disengaged before she actually dropped out. The other student, a male, was actively engaged in sports and other activities at the time of his death. The girl and the school had already started to disengage from each other at the time of her death, and there was no formal postvention response. In the other case, the school and the student had an active relationship that required an elaborate set of postvention responses for teachers as well as students.

Choosing Postvention Response Activities

It is critical to gauge the needs and reactions of those affected by the death and put the response plan into action the day after the death. Postvention is an immediate response and is always done within a few days of the incident.

Observing and listening to students, teachers, and other staff for their expressions of grief, shock, and loss will guide the selection of needed activities. In some cases, only a small group of students who were close associates will require attention, while other incidents seem to deeply touch everyone, including staff and teachers.

Postvention focuses on humanely assisting people with beginning the process to get over a death and helping individuals identify how they are touched and where they need to focus their own recovery. It is not a long-term process, nor is it deep therapy for those with other problems that may have become heightened as a result of the death.

Selecting Personnel to Provide Response Services

School counselors, social workers, and psychologists on staff with appropriate training and interest often provide group and individual services in the postvention response. They have the advantage of under-standing the school, its people, and the culture from the inside. They also know the usual behaviors and strengths of those going through the loss and have ideas about what they will respond to and need. However, incidents may require more services than available school personnel can offer. Many times, members of the school's response team may also be deeply affected by the death and need postvention assistance themselves. Finally, all of those capable members of the team will not be available when the actual need occurs, because of illness, attendance at a training conference, or other reason that has taken them away for a few days.

Some schools have established contracts in advance with community professionals who provide services as needed. In one model, a "post-vention coordinator," who is a trained mental health expert specializing in such services, is called in to provide planning and coordination of the total action response of the school (Leenaars & Wenckstern, 1991, p. 182). In other places, employee assistance programs develop contracts with school districts in advance for response services.

Information and Liaison

One person is designated to provide information to the media and other inquiries from the community. Having one person designated reduces gossip and alternate versions of the incident from forming within the school and by the public. Having one central information source also enhances the possibility of receiving accurate, useful information, because people will then know where to go to obtain it.

It is essential to provide clear, factual information about the death to students the day or early the day after the incident occurs. Some schools have tried to protect students by not providing factual notice or by giving incomplete information in the mistaken belief that young people cannot handle news of tragedy and loss. Postvention theory is based upon hav-ing people experience loss directly and share their feelings, concerns, and questions with others who have shared the event. Experience consistently indicates that children and youth have more difficulty getting through and then later getting over a loss of another through death if others around them refuse to discuss and share feelings and thoughts about it directly. One 11-year-old girl described her experience concerning the recent death of her father. He was originally thought to have committed suicide, but his wife (the girl's stepmother) was later convicted of his murder. When asked how she was able to cope with his death, she replied that her family had dealt with her honestly and factually and with considerable support about the incident. She was emphatic in saying that children should be dealt with directly and not shielded from shocking events within their families or circle of friends that affect them.

Following the Regular School Routine after the Incident

As far as is practical and in good taste, the usual activities of the school should be followed immediately following the death of a school member. Participants in classes and other activities need to be given the opportunity to talk about the death and ask any questions that they may have about circumstances. Lockers, desks, and other personally assigned equipment should remain for a few days. The "empty desk routine" is often used, in which a school counselor follows the schedule of a deceased student the day after the death to answer questions and encourage a brief sharing of feelings and thoughts about the person for a few minutes at the start of the hour.

When school officials have not acknowledged the death afterward or have immediately reassigned desks and wall lockers, students have reacted with frustration. Their opinions were that the deceased person was not respected and that everyone did not get to reflect and comment about the loss and the person being gone.

However, the "empty desk" and other reminders that were the deceased person's should not remain vacant longer than a few days. It is healing and meaningful for people to move ahead and have life go on after a time of respectful acknowledgment and expressing feelings of loss and mourning.

Drop-In Counseling Rooms

The day of and day after the death, counseling rooms may be set aside and made available to staff as well as students who can drop in as needed, individually or in small groups, to talk with someone about their feelings and thoughts concerning the incident. The counselor must be someone who is not so deeply and personally affected by the incident that he or she also needs grief assistance. Counselors must be screened in advance for their comfort with death issues, and it is advisable to provide in-service training for school counselors, social workers, and administrators to prepare them for crisis and grief counseling roles. Frequently, schools will request support service staff from other schools or community professionals to help out with drop-in counseling.

The specific needs of people for immediate grief counseling vary considerably, but generally, they need some emotional catharsis and the chance to talk out the meaning of the death and try to make sense of it for themselves. Frequently, students or staff may ask for practical advice about what to say or do in response to loss by the family and closest associates. In many cases, people visit drop-in services to be with someone while they are in shock or cognitively sorting out their feelings.

Some young people react very strongly and need assistance to get control over their feelings and actions. It is important to allow individuals to express themselves clearly and completely before attempting to help them gain control; otherwise, they may think that their feelings are not acceptable, they are being told how to feel, or the subject is too overwhelming to talk about. After listening patiently and fully, the counselor can then decide if the person needs help with regaining control. Some of the concerns include not being able to stop crying or talking about it, wanting to kill themselves like the suicide victim, or wanting to inappropriately memorialize or immortalize the deceased.

Critical Incident Debriefing

A major element of postvention is the critical incident debriefing conducted by trained personnel with those closely affected by the incident. The principle developer was Jeffrey Mitchell, a counseling psychologist, former firefighter, and emergency medical technician (Mitchell, 1983, pp. 36–39). Over the past few years, the process has been increasingly used in other workplaces and school settings.

In critical incident stress debriefing, a trained debriefing team meets with those directly involved and affected within one to five days of the occurrence.

The principle behind the debriefing process is that certain deaths and other occurrences are too much for people to handle through their normal defenses. In the school setting, a student death, particularly by suicide, is a prime example. The loss of another teacher or other staff member is another seriously felt loss. Multiple casualty situations also add to the shock and grief felt at the school.

It is helpful for those who were part of the same event to share the debriefing as a group to support each other and to try to make sense of it with each other. Participants are encouraged to express any thought and feeling out loud with each other. After free expression, particularly anger or crying, group members are encouraged to regain self-control and move ahead. The formal group debriefing is powerful as a closure ceremony for participants. It provides a time to make full expression of grief and sorrow, acknowledge the loss, and move on at the end of the debriefing. Although neither the debriefing nor the whole postvention experience takes care of the total grief and loss for participants and survivors, it is an important benchmark and source of strength that helps people move on with regular, daily activities and responsibilities.

Determination and Planning Formal Debriefings

Careful planning must be done between the person in charge of the school's postvention plan for the incident and the team member coordinator who will be in charge of the debriefing. The school (requestor) remains in charge of deciding the kinds of debriefing services needed by the debriefing team (provider). It is important for the debriefing coordinator to have specific information about the incident and those involved: What are the facts of the incident? Who were the victims? When did the incident occur? How many people at the school are affected? How are school personnel and students responding now? What other postvention efforts have occurred or have been planned?

The planning phase is obviously necessary to provide needed information to determine the relative severity of the effect of the event and make decisions about response activities.

The process also helps the requestor think through the incident and its effects as well as begin to gain a sense of control over the situation following the occurrence.

Staging the Debriefing

Full cooperation with the standard procedures for debriefings is required for the process to work well.

It should be held at least one day after the incident, after everyone has had at least one cycle of rest, but less than a week from when it happened.

All of those directly involved or affected by the incident should attend the debriefing, even those who say that they do not need it. In our experience, participants who did not think they needed the debriefing almost invariably reported afterward that they did. Their psychological defenses were providing some denial as a shield against shock and loss at the time of the incident.

The physical setting should be a comfortable room with conference tables arranged in a circle or square configuration. The room should afford privacy and freedom from interruptions. If refreshments are available, fruit juice, water, coffee, and cookies are suggested. Alcoholic beverages are not served because they slow the cognitive process and concentration and add to depression. A box of tissues is provided.

Debriefing sessions typically last two to three hours. Participants are expected to plan to remain for the full event without breaks or leaving.

There will be no administrative critique of the incident or its handling by the school, police, medical personnel, or family members of the victims. Although these issues are of highest importance, they should be aired in a different forum or investigation. The focus of critical incident debriefing is on the personal thoughts, feelings, and concerns of individual participants and the group (Deaton & Morgan, 1993).

The following are the steps in a critical incident debriefing.

1. *Introduction.* Team members introduce themselves and describe the process that will be followed for the session. Debriefers do not sit together but are dispersed around the circle.
2. *Rules.* It is explained that material discussed is confidential and that the debriefers do not keep notes on what is said. Everyone is encouraged to speak about anything related to their thoughts and feelings about the incident.
3. *Fact and thought phase.* In the first round, each person is asked to respond in turn with a brief self-introduction including their role and relationship to the incident. If involved in the incident, they are asked to tell what happened. If not involved at the scene, they describe their first thought or reaction when they first heard the news.
4. *Reaction and reflection phase.* After giving every individual a chance to describe their initial involvement, there is a second round of responses invited by the debriefer to elicit each person's response about the worst or most troubling thing about it to them at the time and at the present.

5. *Symptom discussion phase.* Directly following the previous phase, group members begin to offer supportive comments and describe things they do to deal with the grief, loss, and stress from the incident. Participants often talk about positive things that they have done in similar situations.

6. *Teaching phase.* Only after it is clear that all individual expressions have been made by participants, there is a shift to a brief training component. Suggestions are made for dealing with grief, mourning, and stress. Physical, emotional, cognitive, and spiritual components of dealing with the incident are described by the debriefers, and participants often add their own suggestions to the group. Reprinted training materials may be handed out in the educational phase. The end of this phase provides a natural ending point for the debriefing session.

7. *Closure phase.* Questions and other comments are invited by the debriefers, and a summary statement is made. The ending provides a closure point for participants to realize that they have taken action to deal with their initial grief, shock, and mourning in a timely way and with the others who shared it with them.

Follow-Up

Individuals who may still be experiencing upset or other difficulties two to three weeks later with such symptoms as depression, sleeplessness, or obsession with the incident should be identified for follow-up counseling.

The debriefing team contact should check with the school about six weeks after the debriefing for feedback on the quality and usefulness of the debriefing experience for participants.

7

Teaching and Assisting with Grief and Loss

This chapter describes considerations for teachers, administrators, and other professionals in offering counseling and instruction to children, youth, and parents. It begins with the educational component.

CONSIDERATIONS FOR CREATING A SUICIDE PREVENTION AND DEATH ISSUES CURRICULUM IN SCHOOLS

Students in today's schools are familiar with peers who die by suicide, homicide, and accidents, placing the issues of suicide and other death into the school setting, which educators and other adults are not yet comfortable with themselves. In situations where educators and administrators decide not to guide the students to an understanding of death, an opportunity is lost to prepare students for the reality of life and death in an atmosphere where the normal grief reaction can be dealt with in a safe, supportive climate.

When considering how to address the issues of death and suicide in the school, the development of the role of parents needs to be carefully considered. It is imperative that parents be informed of the need to present the information to students and that they be involved in the selection and design of the manner in which it is presented. No student should be forced to participate in classes that are a part of the suicide prevention curriculum if their parents cannot agree with it. The content of suicide prevention and death classes are such that family values and belief systems are involved, and schools need to be sensitive to those systems. Classroom curriculums and teaching methods should be designed to complement the needs of the families in the district and to gain their support.

The goals for a death education and suicide prevention curriculum are:

to present age-appropriate information to students that will allow them to understand the reality of death and its relation to the complete life process;

to provide students with accurate information about the causes and prevention of untimely death, including suicide, accident, and homicide;

to provide students with the assurance that significant adults in their environment, including their parents, are able to answer their questions about death;

to provide students with the developmentally helpful information they need to deal with the death experiences they encounter through the death of family, friends, and school staff; and

to help students to learn about resources and how to access and use them for intervention and postvention assistance (Jackson, 1966; Berkan, 1990; Corr & McNeil, 1986).

Classroom goals should revolve around providing students with information about death issues and about where to go for help for themselves and friends to stop dangerous behavior and handle grief and loss. Religious belief about an afterlife and the morality of the death and suicide issues are best left to the family and the community churches. Selection of the teacher and the grade levels to present the course work are important components basic to the success of the effort. Parental involvement in these decisions is another opportunity to demonstrate the school district's commitment to the preservation of the families. The process by which decisions on content, instructor, and level of presentation are made should be based on consensus between the technical expertise of the educators and the wishes of parents.

A representative committee of parents and other interested community members should meet with the district to achieve a common understanding for the curriculum. The primary task of the committee is to design course work that will achieve the educational goals of the district and be acceptable to the community. The school district must establish two positions clearly from the beginning of the development of the death and suicide prevention curriculum. First, the content will include input developed from open dialogue with the parents. Any parent who wishes should be able to choose to have their student given alternate educational opportunities during any class period that includes death and suicide information. Second, curriculum that deals with suicide or death issues will not focus only on death and suicide. It is prevention oriented and should include information on violence prevention, problem solving, self-esteem, the relation of alcohol and drug abuse to suicide, along with the family and community resources available to help in crisis situations. The preventive value of the curriculum lies in its ability to help students understand how to solve problems and how to ask family, school staff, and community agencies for help.

Much important preventive material is taught in the social studies, human growth and development, and social problems curriculum, and it need not be duplicated in the death issues and suicide prevention curriculum (Bowers et al., 1988). When the material that deals directly with suicide or death is presented by the regular classroom teacher, there is a second school staff person present, who may be another teacher or a pupil service worker (school social worker, school psychologist, school counselor, or school nurse). Staff who present material should be comfortable with it. If the topics stimulate negative emotional reactions in the presenters, the presenters will not be good role models for students dealing with death issues. Presenters should observe the reaction of individual students to the material, because it is natural that some member of the class will have difficulty dealing with it. The adult instructors should be prepared to respond to any distress or lack of understanding they observe on the part of the class members. The adult leaders should talk to any student who appears to be upset or confused about concepts and discover what the problem might be. Students who are upset can meet individually with the second staff person in the class to provide counseling or explanation (Pfeffer, 1989, p. 207). Material on death and suicide can stimulate memories about relatives or friends who have died or may reawaken an individual's own memories of suicidal ideation or action. Although the use of two presenters in the classroom and the availability of a counseling resource in the building during and immediately after the presentation may seem excessive, it is the responsible action to take. If a student is very troubled, the school should discuss the reaction with the student's parents. The sensitivity of the school to its responsibility is an example of the partnership with parents necessary to successfully provide an effective educational experience for students.

Suicide and death information presented as a part of a large assembly program or a one-time workshop must be done carefully. Large assemblies do not allow for staff to observe student reactions or for the students to intellectually process their reaction or gain an understanding of the information by engaging in open discussions lead by a responsible adult. This is possible in a smaller group setting. The large, school-wide presentation to students will be useful only for providing limited information and informing students of the school's intent to provide instruction and assistance in a more detailed way.

STUDENT READINESS FOR THE SUICIDE PREVENTION/DEATH EDUCATION CURRICULUM

Young people are involved in dealing with several issues that must be resolved as they seek maturity. Their maturation and resolution of certain issues determine how they understand death and loss. The developmental issues are attachment (transforming childhood bonds between parents and children), autonomy (extending self-initiated activities), sexuality (transforming social and gender roles to include sexual activity), intimacy (transforming acquaintanceships into deeper friendships), achievement (accenting future-oriented activities), and identity (developing images of self to accommodate complex attributes, including positive self-image and personal competence) (Hill, 1980; Lipsitz, 1980).

In dealing with youth concerning the issues of death and grief from natural causes, accident, or suicide, it is important to consider how young people perceive death and how adults can present information in a helpful manner. Children are faced with death from an early age through the fictionalized deaths of movie or television characters and the actual death of family members or friends. To the child under the age of five, death is the same as sleep or of someone leaving on a long trip. They do not grasp or understand the finality of the death of someone they know. The emotional reaction of significant adults around them will determine how they deal with death and will form the foundation for the more complete understanding that will emerge in later years. From ages five to nine, children achieve a basic understanding of death, but they do not accept its power over them. Death is something that happens to others, not to them. After age nine and extending through adolescence, children can become aware that death happens to everyone, that it is final, and that it is a biological process (Dershimer, 1990; Corr & McNeil, 1986; Bernstein & Gullo, 1977; Carrol, 1985). Educators who are aware of the understanding of children in the developmental stages can use that knowledge to introduce the topic in an appropriate manner.

Meaningful learning about death in the K–12 educational process does not occur only through a specialized course or instructional unit to provide students with the information they need to develop useful understanding. It does require that the teachable moments that occur in all classes and school activities be used to help students understand the meaning of death. Such moments might be during discussions of the fictional death of a character in a story or the real-life death of a family member or friend. When family or friends of students die in car accidents, from violence, or from illness, they will wonder why it happened and what death means to them. If they are comfortable with the adults around them, they may ask questions, and the adults can meet their needs by facilitating the normal grieving process or satisfying their questions. Students who were closest to the deceased will be most affected by the death and will need to resolve the grief before they will be able to function fully in the school setting again.

Not only must responsible adults understand how children view death and how to help them understand the concept more accurately, they must also understand the relationship between suicide prevention curriculums and postvention activities in response to a completed suicide. A common assumption is that postvention is limited to dealing with a crisis situation and insuring that other students do not imitate their classmate through self-destructive actions. A prevention curriculum, on the other hand, is seen as providing students with information and skills that will insulate them from initiating self-destructive behavior. Postvention also provides guidance to the prevention efforts by suggesting areas of focus based on what students need and how they and staff might respond. The prevention imperative to not keep it a secret when a peer has discussed suicide intent is an example of something learned through postvention activities. Prevention focuses on the strengths of the individual, family, friends, the school, and the community that can be used by children and their families.

Postvention focuses on needed efforts in response to a death or other trauma that has already occurred. Individuals are actively sought out and offered help, and friends are sensitized to the possibility of peers needing help and are urged to bring those friends to help. Postvention seeks to normalize the grieving process and return survivors to a new situation where they are able to function without the presence of their deceased friend. Postvention contributes to developing resiliency by demonstrating ways to seek brief, timely assistance to recover from life's traumas and losses.

CONTENT OF THE SUICIDE PREVENTION/DEATH EDUCATION CURRICULUM

The presentation of suicide prevention and death information within the school setting first begins with factual information about the topic. In the case of suicide, the causes and effects of an individual's decision to kill themselves becomes important to share with the class. Students need to understand that the suicide is not an act that occurs spontaneously without prior events. Describing the events that lead up to a suicide attempt can allay fears that their own normal negative thoughts will not necessarily overcome their desire to live. The instructor can provide information about help available that the students can use to provide alternatives to self-destruction.

Next, students must be able to intellectually understand the concepts involved in the material. Death as a normal part of the life process is a concept that individuals must come to accept in order to conduct their life in the manner they believe to be the most appropriate. It is a concept that implies that we need to make choices of how we will make major commitments in life.

Closely connected with intellectual learning is the integration of ideas and skills into the personal lives of students. Formal learning must have importance that will help students view their lives differently and more realistically, and in so doing, they will be able to discover the meaning of life for themselves.

SUICIDE PREVENTION AND DEATH EDUCATION CURRICULUM IN THE CLASSROOM

Classroom presentations need to include and integrate a combination of information on the facts of death, including suicide, and discussion on how to handle the emotions and thoughts for dealing with deaths of all kinds.

Students need to be prepared for ways to respond after the death of someone they know. Students want to know what they can say to someone they know who has suffered a loss, especially through suicide. Most adults do not have the training and experience to know what to say. In fact, students should be told that there is no one right thing to say in these situations. It is important that survivors and friends know that their presence and their concern is the best help they can give. Touching a grieving person is helpful; letting them know that someone is there breaks into the feeling of isolation and reconnects grieving people to the everyday world. At times they may not want to talk very much, while at other times they may wish to have a trusted friend listen to them discuss their feelings and memories.

Students want to know what survivors are thinking and feeling. Much of the information they have comes from peers and the stereotyped responses they have seen depicted in movies or on television. A great deal of this information is inaccurate and confusing to students, and curricular materials can be helpful if they stress that no individual knows what others feel unless they actually share their feelings.

It is common for youth to blame themselves for not preventing the suicide. Friends of suicide victims need to be reminded that suicide is not a common experience that we can always recognize as a danger, and even when friends say they are going to kill themselves, such comments do not always seem serious. Suicide victims who do not share how unhappy they were or how badly they felt could not be helped, because their pain was a secret. Suicide is a choice that some individuals make, and students need to be helped to see the limits of their responsibility for friends who are suicidal.

Grief should be an integral topic in any death issues curriculum. It is natural and represents the realization that a close friend or family member is gone and that the student will miss many experiences that could have been shared further with that person. It is a recognition that something of worth has been lost to survivors and to the world. Students need to be taught that it helps to tell another person who has lost a friend or loved one that they are sorry for the pain the survivor is enduring.

Students should be reminded that there are adults who want to share their grief and help them deal with it because they care for them. Classroom discussion about death and suicide represents one time when the adult concern for youth can be reinforced in the minds of the students. Such assurance of adult interest will have a positive effect on students who are faced with dealing with the death of others. Adults who are concerned about helping students deal with grief need to stress to students that the emotional strain of a death loss has a profound impact on survivors. Caring adults and peers who understand this will not be surprised if a survivor seems preoccupied or if they verbally strike out at those around them. Their adjustment to the loss of their friend or relative through death may take all their physical and emotional energy and leave little to deal with other friends and survivors.

Part of teaching about grief includes helping students understand that grieving people need time and psychological space to resolve their feelings. Although it might be misinterpreted as selfishness on the part of the one suffering the loss and can be hurtful to the friends who are trying to help, teaching students the variety of responses to expect can have a calming effect on the emotional impact of a death or suicide.

The value of sharing real experiences with death and grief by the teacher with students is important. Because we seldom talk about death, students will have both a natural curiosity and a tendency to avoid such personal experiences. Instructors who are able to share what they felt when dealing with death and grief can give students important information about what to expect when they have their own experiences. Teachers should not assume, however, that students will feel the same emotions that they felt in the same manner. They need to be taught that, quite appropriately, they will react and feel in their own way.

It can be demonstrated through classroom discussion and by actions after a suicide that the value of caring people to survivors is helpful in the grieving process. Psychiatrist and suicide survivor Sue Chance describes the message that students need to hear about how they can help survivors they know.

She (a friend) said things . . . things my family had said, but which came from a different direction and thereby were meaningful in a different way. . . . (They say) You hope for the best but you can't control your child's life, it doesn't belong to you. . . . (My) husband comforts me . . . sometimes by leaving me alone, sometimes by talking to me. . . . My co-workers talk to me if I open the subject and don't if I don't. That helps me too. (Chance, 1992)

The literature has many similar first-person accounts by survivors of how they dealt with their grief that can be valuable to students and help them understand how families and friends feel about suicide and how it affected them (Harness-Overley, 1992; Wrobleski, 1991; Kolehmainen & Handwerk, 1986). One of the clear messages in first-person accounts is the discussion of unfounded guilt that survivors must deal with and the pain they endure until they are able to move along the grief process. More academic descriptions of the process emphasize the stages of shock and disbelief, denial, guilt, anger, depression, resolution, and acceptance. However, it is the personal accounts of survivors that show the reality of the process. It is clear from reading their stories that survivors do not progress neatly through the stages of grief but move back and forth between emotional states until they are ready to move on to a more complete resolution of their emotional reaction.

Instruction on the effect of the emotional impact of death on individuals is important. Knowledge that survivors are often unable to think clearly after a death or suicide, that they frequently become depressed themselves, that everyday functioning may be temporarily impaired, and that they may even fight with each other is critical information to share. It is particularly important to stress that it is all natural and that much of it can be resolved by talking it out with each other and with adults who care. Developing a more integrated understanding of grief is essential to the students' ability to deal with loss within their own lives.

Classroom discussion that acknowledges the pleasure and the contributions the deceased student gave to their friends places the situation into perspective. Students who are prepared to evaluate suicide or other deaths in such a manner have a realistic foundation for understanding their own experience and that of other survivors to the loss.

The reorientation of a group to life without the victim is a realistic topic for discussion in class. How activities will be different without their friend places the aftermath of a suicide into perspective for students and emphasizes the fact that life does go on after a death of any kind.

Students must be allowed to say what and how they feel about suicide and those people who commit suicide. Students should be encouraged to realize that talking about death and suicide is healthy, especially if they have recently experienced a loss themselves. The fact that there are adults and friends willing to listen is an important concept to emphasize, because communication between adults and youth is often troublesome and difficult.

Suicide and other deaths create survivors of the victim who have much to resolve. Survivors must face pain, and in the case of suicide, students need to recognize and understand the disturbing feelings of anger they have because their friend left without saying goodbye, without resolving any of the problems they had with each other, and without having the chance to relieve guilt over real or imagined wrongs.

An effective study of suicide or other death deals with the fact that there are not always reasons to explain why a death or a particular suicide occurs. Students need to know that there are some reasons that we may never know. Perhaps a suicidal person was having trouble at home or had a secret they did not want to share. They deserve the dignity of having their wishes for privacy respected. The students should know that suicide happens because the person believes that there is no other way out for them, and though we may disagree strongly, the individual made the decision for reasons of their own. That suicide occurs in healthy families is a fact that should be handled in the class, because it validates the concept that blame over the loss of a friend or loved one is neither productive nor accurate. It is the grief process that allows survivors to find their own answers to a friend's death. Instructors in suicide and other death courses need to acknowledge that most of what we talk about in regard to a friend who died, especially one who has commited suicide, can be interpreted more than one way. Students may remember a comment that might have been a cry for help or that could just have been part of a simple conversation. The message of classroom discussion should include that, as time passes, students will find some answers that will be comforting for them and they will discover that it is possible to eventually accept the fact that we do not have all the answers about why certain deaths occur.

CLASSROOM GUIDELINES

Teachers must know the class members as individuals. Because the occurrence of suicide or other death issues deals with a sensitive topic not often talked about in society, students will approach it with some apprehension. Each of the students in the class will have developed their own concept and emotional response to death. Those responses can range from depression and withdrawal to mysticism and fear to an intellectual curiosity. Experiences each has had with death can affect the students' ability to deal with the class material. Those who have had losses that they have not resolved or who may be considering suicide may react negatively and need assistance with their emotional state to avoid pain or self-destructive behavior. Teachers who are familiar with the normal behavior of individual students will be able to detect significant responses.

The classroom instructor must be a trusted adult. Teachers develop trusting relationships with students, and when difficult topics are discussed this relationship is invaluable in helping students successfully deal with emotionally difficult material. The relationship encourages students to ask critical questions about death and suicide that can be the basis for not only a fuller understanding of death but also an awareness on the student's part that adults are ready to help if they, or a peer, need assistance. If the material is given by a professional who is a stranger, the students are less likely to share their concerns.

The classroom instructor must be comfortable with the subject of death. Teachers and counselors vary in their knowledge, experience, and desire to deal with death issues. Those who present these issues to students should be comfortable with their own feelings and reactions to death, dying, and grief, know the subject matter thoroughly, use death language easily, understand the developmental stages of life, and be aware of the social changes that affect society's approach to death. With a solid knowledge base and the confidence in their ability to deal with their own experiences with death, the teacher can provide information to students and help them understand death sufficiently to cope with any experiences with death they may have.

Presentations should be age appropriate, allow for discussion, and cover a minimum amount of material to insure that full discussion takes place. Death is a topic that is not dealt with effectively on a one-time basis. Knowledge of death is a cumulative experience that involves seeing friends and family die and learning to deal with those losses in an effective manner. Death education does not replace the life experiences in people's lives; it provides another opportunity for students to process the meaning of death and integrate it into reality.

The developmental stage of the student will dictate the amount and form of the topic. Younger children are not ready to fully understand the biological process of death; therefore, technical descriptions of death will be confusing to them. They need to know that death is not something they need to fear and that adults are nearby, protecting them from danger. As students progress and they begin to understand the finality of death, they can be given biological information and can begin to understand that death is a part of the life cycle. In adolescence the reality of death and the family and religious values surrounding death are appropriate for study.

Receptivity to death education is a personal process that each individual completes on his or her own schedule. The teachable moment often becomes more important than the lesson plan. When the teacher might want to discuss burial practices, the class may want to explore why people cry at funerals. What the class wishes to discuss, as long as it is pertinent to the topic of death and death issues, should guide the teacher's decision on class content for a given day. The emotional content of topics surrounding death require that teachers take whatever time is necessary to deal with what concerns students. Scheduling enough time and being flexible about discussions allows the students' needs to be met more adequately. The use of lengthy audio visuals that take up the majority of the available class time is not advisable because it does not allow time to respond to questions and concerns of students that teaching aids stimulate.

Teachers who are planning to present suicide and other death issues in class should prepare themselves not only through reading and course-work but also by consulting professionals who deal with death as a part of their everyday experience. Funeral directors, pastors, and mental health counselors and hospital staff are valuable sources of information that can be used to facilitate student learning in classroom. Community professionals can be invited as guest speakers to allow students to benefit from their special knowledge and experience with people in a variety of grief and loss situations. The inclusion of these professionals in teacher preparation and classroom presentation activities normalizes death as a reality.

Deliberate use of harsh presentations of death situations is avoided in death issues education. Class trips to morgues, watching a body being embalmed, or viewing graphic pictures of violent death are examples of activities that are *not* recommended. Exercises such as writing one's own obituary or visiting a funeral in progress are problematic. Writing one's own obituary may be of value to some students, but in others, it might produce a strong negative reaction. Attendance at a funeral in progress as a class experience is in bad taste because it is probably intrusive on family and friends of the deceased. Designing and implementing a death issues education experience is a task the educator must approach with a sense of balancing the presentation of facts with the emotional impact those facts may have on students.

Pupil service staff must be available to attend class and to talk to certain students afterward who seem upset or have special needs which cannot be handled in a class group. The support staff are valuable as consultants to teachers who are unsure of how a class member may react to the material. In situations where a student may have recently experienced a loss or may have survived a suicide attempt, the pupil services staff can evaluate the potential reaction of that student to the material and help the teacher take appropriate measures to meet the student's needs.

DEALING WITH REACTIONS OF PARENTS AND FAMILIES

Family structures and patterns have been cited as major causes of suicide in children and adults. Pfeffer (1986, pp. 148–49) describes a family system that greatly contributes to suicidal disposition in children. Chapter 5 of this book elaborates on many of the parental and other family influences on suicide and violent tendencies in youth and how school professionals can relate to parents in such families.

However, there are an increasing number of influences outside the family setting that greatly affect suicide and violence in young people.

Factors include media, certain popular music, peer influences, and some school activities that demand high competition levels.

The approach of the school to parents can best begin by taking an open, supportive position that does not assume that suicide or violent behavior of the child had to be caused by the family. Contributing factors to causation from outside the family, including the school's influence, must be evaluated. The school's recommendation for professional treatment for the child or family can be more persuasive with the parents when it is based upon assessment and support rather than preconceived stereotypes about behavior or circumstances.

All professionals working directly with the family where a death has occurred must convey the understanding that there has been a profound loss. Family treatment experts and postvention authorities both emphasize the difference between profound loss and grief and psychopathology (Everstine et al., 1993, pp. 49–59; Mitchell & Bray, 1990, pp. 9–14). The first efforts must be directed toward the recovery by family members from the trauma of death or serious suicide attempt. Trauma, shock, and grief are normal responses to abnormal events that parents and families cannot be expected to handle easily or totally within their own resources. Reactions to a death or other traumatic event are not the same as mental illness or family dysfunctional behavior. In cases where there are family problems such as violence, abuse, or mental illness, the loss and grief must be handled first before moving to problem behavior of the family or its members.

The school's plan for managing death issues must consider the limits of services that the school will agree to offer the family and its members other than the child who is a student at the school. At the least, the school will establish procedures and designate responsible staff to contact the family following a suicide attempt or death of a student as part of the postvention plan. The school intervention plan will include, as a minimum, procedures for referral services to parents and families when their sons or daughters are suicidal or violent or have other serious personal difficulties that school counseling and social work services are not equipped to address.

The strongest support that schools offer students and their families lies in being consistently dependable and available in daily educational and activity programming. Wallerstein and Kelly (1981) in their study of children in divorce found that students consistently listed the school as their greatest resource and support during times of family disruption. Benard (1991) and others, in describing resilient children and youth, cite the dependability and availability of the school and its staff as a principal support for vulnerable young people. The authors' experience as parents and as professionals working with suicidal students and the schools finds the regular activities of the school and the daily contact by a variety of school staff to be the strongest resource and support for students. Often, schools do not realize how positively they are viewed by student families because parents tend to voice their complaints about something the school is doing or not providing more often than they verbalize their satisfaction with other activities. Also, students with the most severe problems tend to be from families who resist intervention from schools and other community services. For most families in the neighborhood and community, the school is seen as a powerful resource as well as an important part of the growth and future of their children.

8

Summary and Future Implications

The development of a comprehensive plan by the school is the key to effective programming in prevention, intervention, and postvention. In our experience, developing the most workable plan possible at the time is more important than delaying implementation until a perfect and complete plan can be approved. Because urgent needs for intervention and postvention services will come without warning, plans and designated personnel for crisis response must be the first priority. Components that require school board review, development, and collaboration of other community agencies can be considered later in the total plan.

Schools and communities will vary in the kinds of plans they will be able to develop. Some local areas see greater urgency than others in allocating resources based on such factors as the incidence of teen suicide or violence in their towns and neighborhoods and the experience of parents, community agencies, and schools working together. The availability of money, personnel, and time are also different from one area to the next. Urban and rural areas are contrasted by demographics and the mix of formal resources for collaboration and referral. Some rural schools develop plans with nearby communities for cooperative assistance, particularly with postvention services. Others develop contracts with specialists in urban centers for specific services in curriculum and program development. Community educational and social service leaders are beginning to develop an array of partnership programs for reducing youth suicide and other high risk behaviors of students (Melaville & Blank, 1993).

DEVELOPING A COMPREHENSIVE PLAN

Many sources are available that serve as guides and models for developing school/community plans, but all we have reviewed are specialized and deal, respectively, with prevention, intervention, or postvention plans. Some focus on crisis response and include plans for intervention and postvention.

The following are practical sources for each component that we recommend.

Prevention

Benard, Bonnie. 1991. *Fostering Resiliency In Schools.* Western Regional Center for Drug Free Schools and Communities, 101 NW Main, Suite 500, Portland, OR 97204.

Berkan, William. 1986. *Suicide Prevention: A Resource and Planning Guide.* Wisconsin Department of Public Instruction, Madison, WI.

Deaton, Robert, and Daniel Morgan. 1992. *Managing Death Issues in the Schools, Monograph No. 1.* Montana Office of Public Instruction, Helena, MT.

Comprehensive Planning

McWhirter, J. Jeffries, et al. 1993. *At Risk Youth: A Comprehensive Response.* Brooks/Cole Publishing Company, Pacific Grove, CA.

Melaville, Atelia, and Martin J. Blank. 1993. *Together We Can: A Guide for Crafting a Profamily System of Education and Human Services.* U.S. Departments of Education and Health and Human Services, U.S. Government Printing Office, Mail Stop: SSOP, Washington, DC 20402-9328.

Intervention

Galusha, Richard. n.d. *Omaha Student Suicide Prevention and Intervention Programs.* Psychological Services, Omaha Public Schools, Omaha, NE.

Ogden, Evelyn and Vito Germinario. 1988. *The At Risk Student.* Technomic Publishing Company, Lancaster, PA.

Postvention

Johnson, Kendall. 1993. *School Crisis Management*. Hunter House Publishers, Alameda, CA.

Southwest Regional Laboratories. 1993. *Crisis Management in the Schools*. Reprinted by Montana Office of Public Instruction, Helena, MT.

In addition to the sources listed specifically for developing the major components of the school plan, Appendix A, which follows this chapter, provides the most useful tools with which we are acquainted. The References is much more extensive and contains some theoretical and research references that are of more specialized interest.

GENERAL SCOPE AND MISSION

Schools will need to first determine the mission, scope, and range of their plans. The array of services to be offered by the school, training for staff, legal liability considerations, and referral to other agencies all require planning and decision.

Previous chapters have described services and curriculum possibilities for prevention, intervention, and postvention. Schools have always been under pressure to increasingly provide developmental and social services to protect children and youth, to help them develop, and to provide instruction. The authors believe that the school has an essential role but that death issues are clearly the shared responsibility of the family, the school, other community entities, and students themselves.

Schools generally begin by assembling a committee to develop a statement of the mission and goals and a set of objectives. The initial planning group can be strengthened by including interested parents and students. Children, youth, and parents are the ones who know whether planned activities and the way they are delivered meet their needs. Because death education is a developing field, family members have much to contribute to current professional knowledge.

Questions of school responsibility and legal liability must be addressed. Although no person or organization can be totally protected from an attempted lawsuit in an activity involving the school, legal liability of the district and its staff can be reduced to a minimum. We have mentioned previously that educational institutions can eliminate most legal problems by having a comprehensive school plan for intervention and postvention and training school staff in its implementation.

At the present, it appears that the legal threat is a two-edged sword. Because more schools have developed action plans, those few who have not initiated any response are vulnerable because they are doing nothing about obvious needs of students for suicide intervention services and programs to prevent crises and offer trauma recovery services following a death at the school. School responsibility is mitigated to a great degree because its primary focus is on education rather than therapy or medical treatment, such as a hospital or mental health clinic would provide (McWhirter, 1993, p. 298). Therefore, schools are not completely responsible for stopping suicide or eliminating other high risk behavior, but they may be required to make reasonable efforts to intervene, warn parents, and make referrals.

COMMUNITY AND SCHOOL PLANNING

The school may join with other youth and family agencies in the community to develop additional services, particularly in the area of prevention.

Several years ago, one of the authors did an extensive survey of counseling and therapy services for suicide, trauma, and crisis within his own local community with the assistance of a team of university students. He found that some experienced family and youth counselors did not do crisis work after business hours or had no experience with death issues, trauma recovery, or grief with young people or their families. Fortunately, an adequate number were found who did, and a referral roster was prepared and sent to all schools and youth agencies in town.

Community planning can yield possibilities for existing services to be orchestrated in a combined effort in ways that can yield more results and also provide a tangible demonstration of community support to its youth. There are several planning questions which we have found useful.

Can an existing activity be modified to assist in a designated activity for death issues management? Drug and alcohol prevention programs for youth, for example, can include a component on suicide intervention and prevention. Although the number of youth who have attempted suicide is relatively small, the number who have thought about it is high, and most youths know someone who has tried or seriously thought about killing themselves. Educational events and support groups provide good access to high risk youth.

Can social agencies or private therapists and counselors modify time schedules or program options to expand existing services? By offering to be open one evening or early morning per week, agencies could reach more families, particularly those in which the parents work full time. Some programs that have traditionally focused on recreation and development, such as Campfire and 4-H, have changed their program mix to include social skills and personal independence training for children.

How can service clubs be tapped to provide funds or develop programs within their program goals? Virtually all service clubs, fraternal organizations, and some veterans' groups include programs to promote healthy child development or assist youth at risk. Too often they are approached only for money for some new program that the members may not understand or in which they have little interest. They can also be asked to join in with planning, volunteer staffing, and advocating for broader financial support of new efforts.

In all professional efforts to combine or collaborate in offering services by school or community agencies, care must be taken to develop an approach that will actually prevent or alleviate the problem and is respectful of the ways people use and benefit from help. Recent research on at-risk youth points toward the need for greater specificity in matching needs with individualized interventions (Benard, 1991; Frymier, 1992, pp. 47–61; McWhirter et al., 1993, pp. 207–26). Many past efforts have missed the mark simply because they attempt to fit a preconceived, favorite intervention of the adult community with an identified youth problem.

After a full inventory is made of existing services and reasonable modification of programs and service patterns using current resources, the development of new programs can begin. Community support is more likely to be available if the previous step of maximizing existing resources has been accomplished.

BENEFITS FOR SCHOOLS

Planning and taking action to prevent, intervene, and provide postvention services in death situations involving the school have several benefits for the educational system.

It is the authors' position that providing a humane and respectful response with those directly affected by death or the threat of death is the first important reason to develop comprehensive programming. Related to a caring response is that by taking action, students and their families can see that schools care and demonstrate that they want their students to live. Death, grief, and mourning are not handled well by many adults in society, and children need to experience respectful, caring responses by adults following a death of someone close to them.

As a practical matter, it will take less time to manage death and other crisis incidents if the school has invested time and other resources to develop a plan for dealing with them. It is human nature to believe that the incident always happens somewhere else or that there is not time for contingency planning or prevention curriculum because of everyday demands of schools that are more immediate. However, it takes much more time and it is more stressful on everyone to struggle through an emergency with nothing in place.

Comprehensive efforts toward death issues management consider the needs of staff as well as students in a crisis situation. Until recently, the needs of faculty, administrators, and other school staff were not considered following a death of a child. It is now generally recognized that adult professionals need brief trauma recovery assistance through critical incident debriefings to help them return to previous levels of functioning (Mitchell & Bray, 1990).

Finally, the death issues curriculum, the postvention response plan, and the intervention and referral approaches all work together as part of the effort to educate the whole child. The result can produce children and youth who are resilient and can conceptualize and employ positive solutions in lieu of suicide, violence, and other negative behaviors.

EVALUATING RESULTS AND EFFECTIVENESS

Much of the work done until now is characterized as minimal and done as a one-time response to a single crisis event. The efforts of the adult community have often come from a desire to do something that is sometimes hastily conceived but sincerely motivated to help or protect youth without regard for effectiveness or reaching the target for prevention of suicide and other destructive behavior.

Kalafat, Elias, and Berman offer a thoughtful critique of programs and attempt to evaluate them in *Suicide Prevention in Schools* (Leenaars & Wenckstern, 1991, pp. 231–55). They suggest beginning with clear goals and objectives of the program so that a matching evaluation procedure can be developed. A target population of children or youth must be specified for the program and its goals. Efforts directed at all the students in every circumstance tend to have little effect on the problem addressed and may add further confusion in the minds of some children. For example, those educators planning a suicide prevention education program for students must decide if they plan to reach suicidal youth or nonsuicidal individuals who need information to recognize and refer suicidal peers to counseling. One type of postvention program can be directed to those individuals who were closest to the deceased, while another effort might be directed to all students at the school where the incident occurred.

As schools begin to develop more programs in areas of prevention, intervention, and postvention, replicating similar programs in other places to validate effectiveness becomes possible. Fortunately, more programs are being written comprehensively with detailed suggestions for implementation, which makes more exacting replication possible.

Little is known at present about the effect of comprehensive programming of the sort suggested by this book, nor do we know whether one of the three components of prevention, intervention, or postvention is more helpful and understandable to students than others. Evaluation of prevention efforts, particularly in curriculum areas, will take several years of follow-up study with students who have participated in it to determine the effects.

POSSIBILITIES AND THE FUTURE

The authors decided to write this book because we could see many developments in managing death issues that began over 20 years ago coming together in several areas. The schools have moved from not taking action to becoming interested in comprehensive approaches. We are hopeful about combining death issues management with emerging knowledge about the at-risk child and youth as one component of strengthening resiliency. Children who can understand and cope with death situations can have a sense of thriving in spite of adversity and unexpected disappointment. The recent growing trend for schools and other community agencies to come together over a common understanding of child and family problems is promising. The work by Frymier (1992) and Melaville and Blank (1993) indicates that comprehensive school, community, and family approaches can take us very far in solving pressing child and youth problems.

More than anything else, we were motivated to put together a resource that schools and communities could use that brings together our experience and the most useful sources that describe successful practices for planning and managing the array of death issues. Hopefully, our work can also be useful to those who build upon the information and concepts we have presented for future development.

APPENDIXES

Appendix A:
Sources

Written and audio visual sources that are particularly useful for designing a school plan have been selected. Appropriate national organizations that focus on important areas of prevention, intervention, and postvention are listed.

DEVELOPING SCHOOL GUIDELINES

Berkan, William. 1986. *A Guide to Curriculum Planning in Suicide Prevention*. Bulletin No. 6517, Wisconsin Department of Public Instruction, P.O. Box 7841, Madison, WI 53707-7841.

Deaton, Bob, and Dan Morgan. 1992. *Managing Death Issues in the School*. Monograph Series No. 1, Montana Office of Public Instruction, State Capitol, Helena, MT 59620

Galusha, Richard. n.d. *Omaha Student Suicide Prevention and Intervention Programs*. Psychological Services, Omaha Public Schools, 3819 Jones St., Omaha, NE 68105.

Leenaars, Antoon, and Susanne Wenckstern (Eds.). 1991. *Suicide Prevention in Schools*. Hemisphere Publishing Corporation, 1900 Frost Rd., Suite 101, Bristol, PA 19007.

PREVENTION AND INTERVENTION CURRICULUM

Berkan, William. 1990. *A Guide to Curriculum Planning in Suicide Prevention*. Bulletin No. 0500, Wisconsin Department of Public

Instruction, P.O. Box 7841, Madison, WI 53707-7841.

Bernstein, Jo Anne. 1977. *Books to Help Children Cope with Separation and Loss.* R. R. Bowker, New Providence, NJ.

Polly, Joan. 1986. *Preventing Teenage Suicide.* Human Sciences Press, New York, NY.

Smith, Judie. 1989. *Suicide Prevention: A Crisis Intervention Curriculum for Teenagers and Young Adults.* Learning Publications, Holmes Beach, FL.

Zalaznik, Patricia. 1992. *Dimensions of Loss and Death Education: Curriculum and Resource Guide.* 3rd ed. (Also contains *Student Activity Work Book.*) Edu-Pac, 15655 40th Avenue North, Plymouth, MN 55446.

INTERVENTION

Deaton, Bob, and Dan Morgan. 1990. *Intervention Hand Out Packet on Teen Suicide.* Department of Social Work, University of Montana, Missoula, MT 59812.

Everstine, Dianne, and Louis Everstine. 1993. *The Trauma Response: Treatment for Emotional Injury.* W. W. Norton Co., New York, NY.

Human Relations Media. *Suicide Prevention: A Teacher Training Program.* (Available in VHS or 35mm slide format), Human Relations Media, 175 Tompkins Ave., Pleasantville, NY 10570-9973.

Patros, Phillip, and Tonia Shamoo. 1989. *Depression and Suicide in Children and Adolescents.* Allyn and Bacon, New York, NY.

POSTVENTION

Jones, Melinda, and Lisa Paterson. 1993. *Preventing Chaos in Times of Crisis.* Monograph Series No. 2. Montana Office of Public Instruction, State Capitol, Helena, MT 59620.

Johnson, Kendall. 1993. *Crisis School Management.* Hunter House Inc., P.O. Box 2914, Alameda, CA 94501-0914.

Mitchell, Jeff, and Grady Bray. 1990. *Emergency Services Stress.* (Continuing Education Series.) Prentice Hall, Inc. Englewood Cliffs, NJ.

ORGANIZATIONS

American Society of Suicidology, 2459 Ash St., Denver, CO 80222

Association for Death Education and Counseling, 638 Prospect Ave, Hartford, CT 06105-4298

International Critical Incident Stress Foundation, 5018 Dorsey Hall Dr., Suite 104, Ellicott City, MD 21042

National Association of Social Workers, 7981 Eastern Ave., Silver Spring, MD 20910

National Education Association, 1201 Sixteenth St. N.W., Washington, DC 20036-3290

National Committee on Youth Suicide Prevention, 65 Essex Rd., Chestnut Hill, MA 02167

Appendix B:
Examples of a School's Plan

WILLIAMS BAY PUBLIC SCHOOL SUICIDE
PREVENTION — INTERVENTION PLAN
JUNE 29, 1988

Filed with the Department of Public Instruction, July 1, 1988
Wisconsin Department of Public Instruction

The specific inclusion of both education and health and social services agencies in the legislation is a clear indication of the need for cooperation and collaboration at state, regional, and local levels to reduce youth suicide.

PREVENTION: SUICIDE AWARENESS CURRICULUM

The Suicide Prevention Curriculum at Williams Bay School is a K–12 comprehensive program. Following is listed the information and skills taught and the respective grade levels.

Curriculum areas elementary level:

1. K–6 classroom teachers
2. Art
3. Physical Education

The material in this appendix used by permission of the Wisconsin Department of Public Instruction, Madison, Wisconsin.

4. Reading
5. Speech
6. Music
7. Special Education
8. Classroom Guidance

Curriculum areas high school level:

1. Social Studies
2. Math
3. English
4. Science
5. Spanish
6. Reading
7. Physical Education
8. Art
9. Business
10. Music
11. Home Economics
12. Classroom Guidance

Specific curriculum to detect depression or suicidal tendencies are taught in following areas:

Elementary Level:

1. Classroom Guidance
2. Classroom teachers
3. Sixth and Seventh Grade Art and Reading

High School Level:

1. Social Studies
2. Science
3. English
4. Junior High Guidance

Decision-making skills:

Elementary Level:

1. Classroom Guidance
2. Classroom Teachers

3. Art
4. Physical Education
5. Reading
6. Special Education

High School Level:

1. Junior High Guidance
2. Physical Education
3. Science
4. Spanish
5. English
6. Art
7. Social Studies
8. Home Economics
9. Business
10. Math
11. Industrial Arts
12. Music Departments

Information on the conditions that may cause depression or suicide:

Elementary Level:

1. Classroom Guidance

High School Level:

1. Art
2. Social Studies
3. English
4. Junior High Guidance

The relationship between youth suicide and the use of alcohol or other drugs — primarily covered through groups in the student assistance program; at the high school level, information also is provided through classroom guidance and the Social Studies and English departments.

Information on community resources:

Elementary Level:

1. Classroom Guidance

High School Level:

1. Junior High Classroom Guidance
2. Physical Education
3. English
4. Home Economics
5. School Newspaper

Instruction on communication skills:

Elementary Level:

1. Classroom Guidance
2. Classroom Teachers
3. Art
4. Physical Education
5. Reading
6. Special Education

High School Level:

1. Junior High Classroom Guidance
2. Student Assistance Program
3. Reading
4. Spanish
5. Physical Education
6. Science
7. English
8. Art
9. Home Economics
10. Math
11. Business
12. Social Studies

IDENTIFICATION — REFERRAL — ASSESSMENT

Identification: Adults who care about kids need to realize that some of the signs of depression and suicide are normal mood swings and are not unexpected for the maturing young person. The signs become more important when coupled with positive or negative events that are potentially stressful for children, such as:

Personal Stressors:

1. Serious injury or physical/medical disability
2. Alcohol, drug, or emotional problem by student or by their parent(s)
3. Death of a close friend or loss of significant relationship
4. Parents' divorce, separation, or marital discord
5. Pregnancy/becoming a parent
6. Legal trouble
7. Difficulties with boyfriend/girlfriend
8. Beginning or ending a job
9. Christmas season
10. Beginning to date
11. Outstanding personal achievement

Family Stressors

1. Death of parents or sibling
2. Serious illness or injury of family member
3. Parents separating or getting back together
4. Divorce of parents
5. New stepmother or stepfather
6. New stepbrother or stepsister
7. Birth or adoption of sister or brother
8. Brother or sister leaves home
9. Family arguments
10. Family violence and/or physical/sexual abuse
11. Parental chemical dependency
12. Lack of family support
13. Financial difficulties
14. Move to new house

Education Stressors

1. Skipping a grade or staying back a grade
2. Change in schools

3. Trouble with teacher
4. Failure in a course
5. First year of middle school or junior high
6. First and last year of high school
7. Test or exams
8. Not making an extracurricular activity

Signs of depression and suicide become significant when the student feels:

Hopeless: A feeling of being unable to regain control of his or her life or that something will always be in the way of accomplishing goals.
Helpless: A feeling of not having the ability, strength, or intelligence to solve dilemmas.
Hapless: Seeming to float from crisis to mini-disaster to disaster without being able to avoid those situations.

Identifying signs of these states may include:

sadness, the blues
self-blaming
feeling of worthlessness
slower-than-normal speech pattern
sudden change in appetite
weight loss without dieting
headaches, constipation
stomachaches, dizziness
problems breathing
restless feeling
withdrawal from friends, family, and "regular" activities
lack of concentration
physical or emotional fatigue
nervous gestures (tugs hair, rubs skin, pacing)
loss of interest in or unusual neglect of personal appearance
giving away of prized possessions or "putting life in order"
use of drugs or alcohol
themes in thinking that include wanting to join a deceased person, manipulate or punish others, be punished, control death when it comes, become a martyr
comments such as: "I won't be a problem much longer." "Nobody needs me." "I wish I were dead."
noticeable change in eating and sleeping habits
persistent boredom or apathy

sudden, forced cheerfulness after a period of depression
running away
change in quality of school work
violent or rebellious behavior
crying
preoccupation with death
impulsive behavior showing poor judgment: drunk driving, playing "chicken"
accident proneness, promiscuity, self-mutilation
expression of thoughts of despair
recent loss of girlfriend, boyfriend, pet, parent
death of someone close
failure on a test, in sports, or in another extracurricular activity

The key seems to be how the child handles the stress represented by the signs. The above behaviors are not, in themselves, indicative of suicidal ideation. Concern is warranted when more than one sign is observed, change in characteristic pattern of behaviors is noted, the change persists over time, and behaviors are displayed with unusual intensity.

Staff Referral — If any staff member suspects a student may attempt, complete, or is in the process of making a suicide attempt, the staff person is to notify a member of the Crisis Intervention Team immediately. A few things to remember relative to referrals are:

A. Take clues and statements seriously.
B. DO NOT attempt to handle the situation alone. Get Help! Share this information with Crisis Intervention Team members.
C. DO NOT allow yourself to be sworn to secrecy by the student.
D. Ask students to name two people they can trust and talk to. Direct students to one of these resource persons and provide the names of the Crisis Intervention Team members.
E. If you feel the student may be in imminent danger, DO NOT leave the student alone FOR ANY AMOUNT OF TIME!
F. Wisconsin law (s. 895.48) protects from civil liability any person who, in good faith, refers a student for being potentially suicidal.

Assessment — The Crisis Intervention Team or an available member of the Crisis Intervention Team will assess risk factors. The SAL method is typically used in assessing risk.

A. Specificity of the Plan: How specific is the person's suicide plan?
B. Availability of Means: How available is the method chosen to commit suicide? If they have decided to use a gun, for example, and they are from a

family who hunts, the risk is high.
C. Lethality of Method: How lethal is the method chosen? If they plan to use a gun or to hang themselves, for example, the risk is very high.

In general, three categories are and will be used by the Crisis Intervention Team members to potentially suicidal persons.

A. Low Risk
   Criteria:
   1. Vague, general unhappiness
   2. Talk about suicidal thoughts but have low SAL assessment
   3. Issue of suicide is one to be considered but is probably best dealt with by concentrating on the resolution of other problems
   Action:
   1. Monitor student
   2. Provide supportive counseling
   3. Parents should be notified to be a resource if possible
B. Medium Risk
   Criteria:
   1. Vague threats that life is not worth living
   2. Focus on suicide as a solution to problems but have either no plan or a very vague one
   3. Lack of strong support system
   4. Other factors that might be present:
      a. Change in personality or mood swings
      b. Student has given away possessions
      c. Anniversary of a loss
      d. Recent loss
      e. Suicide in the family
      f. Chemical use/abuse
      g. History of suicide preoccupation
      h. Access to death instrument(s)
      i. Signals of stress: anxiousness, inability to concentrate, poor sleeping or eating habits
   Action:
   1. Contact parent unless to do so would not be in the best interest of the student, in which case...
   2. Request assessment from prevention staff at Lakeland Counseling Center and/or...
   3. Call Department of Social Services Protective Services Unit
   4. Advise other members of the Crisis Intervention Team. If suicide threats by the student continue and the parent(s) have been contacted but have not sought professional help, then steps two and three will be followed.

C. High Risk — Lethal
  Criteria:
  1. Student has a specific suicide plan.
  2. Student has access to death implements.
  3. Student has made a written statement about suicide plans.
  4. Student has told another of their specific suicide plan.
  5. Student has made a previous attempt.
  6. Other factors stated above may be present.
  Action:
  1. KEEP THE STUDENT WITH A RESPONSIBLE ADULT AT ALL TIMES.
  2. Inform the student's parents of the situation and advise them of the need for referral. If the danger is high, proceed immediately to the next step.
  3. If necessary, call emergency medical service.
  4. Call Lakeland Counseling Center and ASK FOR EMERGENCY ASSISTANCE.
  5. STAY WITH THE STUDENT until rescue squad, Lakeland Counseling Center personnel, or parents arrive.
  6. Follow up the referral by making direct contact with the student as soon as possible to express interest, concern, and continued acceptance.

PROCEDURE IN THE EVENT OF IN-SCHOOL SUICIDE ATTEMPT

1. Follow "Code Blue" procedures to insure physical well-being.
2. Refer to steps of "Procedure in the Event of a Sudden Death" for procedures.

PROCEDURE IN THE EVENT OF A SUDDEN DEATH

1. The elementary and high school principals have been designated as Crisis Intervention Team Leaders and will be notified as soon as possible. They will work to channel all incoming and outgoing information, make all necessary medical contacts, and represent the school in contacts with the affected family. The Crisis Intervention Team Leaders will also contact all faculty and support staff members, using the emergency telephone network if a death occurs during nonschool hours.

2. The Crisis Intervention Team, consisting of team leader (2), school counselors (2), school psychologist (1), an elementary and high school teacher (2), and a recordkeeper (1), will meet to assess student and staff

needs, to schedule a faculty meeting, to determine the need for outside assistance (Lakeland Counseling Center, Eastern Suburban Conference Counselors, Community Members), to establish a crisis/support center in the schools, and to frame initial public statements.

3. All faculty will attend a special meeting prior to the beginning of classes. The purpose of the meeting will be to review the situation, provide appropriate factual information, compose a prepared statement to be announced to the student body, and to explain the day's agenda, as well as to allow staff to ask questions, begin to deal with their own emotions, and request substitutes if necessary. Outreach personnel will be appointed and assigned time to designated areas (bathroom, locker rooms, hallways).

4. Teachers will provide support to students upon their arrival to school, try to dispel rumors, and, in the event of a suicide, attempt to deglamorize the event. They will advise students where they can go to discuss their feelings and encourage students to be understanding of others' feelings. Outreach personnel will provide support and direction. The Crisis/Support Center will work with individuals needing support and will try to identify high risk students.

5. ALL ATTEMPTS SHOULD BE MADE TO RETURN TO NORMAL AS SOON AS POSSIBLE. No building-wide announcement or large group school assembly will be made or held.

6. Parents will be notified of services available in the school to address grief issues.

7. A second faculty meeting will be held at the end of the day to discuss the day's intervention.

8. The Crisis Team will meet to formulate next day follow-up strategies and to identify high risk students requiring additional support. This may include individual or small group follow-up using both in-school and community resources. If it is determined that "short-term" assistance is needed from the Eastern Suburban Conference Counselor's Association, district administrators from the appropriate school district will be contacted.

9. ALL ATTEMPTS WILL BE MADE TO AVOID CANCELING CLASSES! If visitation or funeral services occur during school hours, students wishing to attend must have parental permission to attend, students must sign out before leaving the school building, and this list will be monitored. Parents will be encouraged to accompany and support their children in attending these activities.

POSTVENTION: PREVENTING
THE CLUSTER EFFECT

1. A follow-up letter to parents will be sent three days after the crisis and/or funeral.

2. Within two weeks of the crisis, the Crisis Intervention Team will meet to review student body, individual student, and staff needs. Additionally, the Crisis Intervention Team may wish to meet with personnel utilized from the community or from the Eastern Suburban Conference Counselors Association to evaluate response and intervention effectiveness.

3. There should be further contact as necessary with students considered to be at risk, particularly at critical periods (one month, three months, six months) or dates (birthdays, anniversary of death, etc.). All students who visited the Crisis Support Center should be monitored.

Appendix C:
Examples of Prevention
Curriculum

INTENDED USE OF THIS GUIDE

The task force developed this guide to meet the curriculum requirements of 1985 Wisconsin Act 29, s. 115.365. This curriculum guide was designed to be used by a local suicide prevention curriculum committee or team responsible for the development, implementation, and evaluation of the local program. It is not a mandated course of study but it may be used as the foundation for a specific instruction program. The authors believe that the philosophy, goals, objectives, and other materials found in this publication will be useful as local districts change, redesign, or otherwise evaluate their current instructional approach to youth suicide prevention.

INITIAL QUESTIONS

Educators should address the following questions when presenting a suicide prevention curriculum.

This appendix is taken from William Berkan. 1990. *A Guide to Curriculum Planning in Suicide Prevention.* Wisconsin Department of Public Instruction, Madison, WI, pp. 6, 7, 12, 13, 18–32 (used by permission).

Why should information about suicide be included in the school curriculum?

Statistics from DPI and Department of Health and Social Services indicate a serious problem. In Wisconsin, deaths of about 60 school-aged youth are reported annually as suicides. Suicide is a leading cause of death for adolescents between the ages of 15 and 19 in Wisconsin and in the rest of the United States.

Early intervention with depressed children may prevent the problem from worsening.

Studies have identified childhood depression as an increasing cause of youth suicide, according to American Association of Suicidology. Many school-aged youth become seriously depressed and require treatment at some point in their school careers according to these studies. Early intervention with depressed children may prevent the problem from worsening. Students often do not seek help on their own or recognize their own depression.

Who should teach this curriculum?

Teaching this curriculum requires no special degree. Inservice training can provide the classroom teachers with a good working knowledge of suicide prevention. Rapport with the age group being worked with and a sensitivity to the emotional reactions of students are essential. *Teachers who are uncomfortable with the subject should not be required to teach the curriculum, since they may communicate their discomfort to students.*

The task force encourages staff members along with community agencies and pupil services to present information as a team with the classroom teacher. In addition, the classroom teacher should have an assistant to ensure a thorough observation of individual students. Individuals with special training in areas such as social work, psychology, nursing, or school counseling can help the classroom teacher in presenting this information to students. The Wisconsin Developmental Guidance Model, the Social Work and Problem Solving Centered Model, and the Psychological Development approach are all appropriate resources for implementing the Suicide-Prevention Curriculum. Information about these resources is available from the DPI's Bureau of Pupil Services. The DPI's *Guide to Curriculum Planning in*

Health Education has a mental and emotional health component which covers much of what the law requires on this subject. The task force also encourages teachers to volunteer to teach suicide prevention in conjunction with their regular subject area. For example, English, family living, psychology, health, and sociology teachers, and teachers of the emotionally disturbed have presented suicide prevention information in the past. Although districts have several options in placing this curriculum, they should offer it in a required class to ensure that all students benefit from it.

Should districts contract with outside experts to present suicide prevention information to the student body?

The DPI discourages using experts who are not well known *and* trusted in the district. Most areas of the state now have local district or community agency people who are capable of making good suicide prevention presentations in a class context or in smaller groups that allow students to discuss the material freely. The use of classroom teachers, pupil services staff, and local community agency staff allows students to meet and speak to the adults who are routinely available to help them. The DPI has and maintains an updated list of persons from throughout the state who can help districts in the area of suicide prevention.

The DPI recommends that educators make suicide prevention presentations in a class context or in smaller groups that allow students to discuss the material freely.

At what age should students be introduced to the suicide prevention curriculum?

This suicide prevention curriculum is designed for use within the K–12 curriculum. It deals with positive emotional development, good communication, coping- and decision-making skills, recognizing suicidal signs in one's self or others, and ways to obtain help. The task force designed the curriculum to introduce topics at an appropriate developmental level; but although the curriculum begins in kindergarten, it does not address suicide directly until the sixth grade. Table 1 on pages 158 and 159 shows the topics included in the guide and the developmental level at which they are addressed.

How do educators develop a "working knowledge" of the topic of suicide?

This curriculum guide contains the basic information needed to teach suicide prevention. It also contains a glossary of terms and graded resource lists for each grade to help obtain additional information. The DPI also published a program guide entitled *Suicide Prevention: A Resource and Planning Guide*, which was distributed to all public school districts. Additional copies are available from the DPI, Publications Sales Office, P.O. Box 7841, 125 S. Webster Street, Madison, WI 53707.

Should districts involve parents when planning to present the suicide-prevention curriculum?

The task force highly recommends that districts include parents and representatives of community agencies when planning implementation of the suicide prevention curriculum. Parents with children involved in the program should preview the suicide-prevention curriculum prior to its delivery.

> *The task force highly recommends that districts include parents and representatives of community agencies when planning implementation of the suicide prevention curriculum.*

Does the DPI offer additional help to teachers and districts in implementing the suicide prevention curriculum and establishing a suicide prevention program?

For technical assistance, contact the Bureau for Pupil Services at 125 S. Webster Street, P.O. Box 7841, Madison, WI 53707, or (608) 266-8960. Additional help may be obtained from local CESA or community agencies. Before implementing a suicide prevention curriculum, it is recommended that educators compile a list of resource agency phone numbers should they need to refer any students.

SAMPLE LESSONS TO IMPLEMENT UNIT (K–12)

These sample lessons on self-esteem highlight the relationship between how individuals feel about themselves and what others feel about them. Throughout the lessons discussions and activities are used to help students learn how to build and maintain a positive self-image. When presenting the lessons, it is important to stress that there are many ways to build self-image so that students will realize that if one doesn't work another is available. This unit forms the foundation for helping students learn how to deal with life problems and avoid suicide.

TABLE 1

Suicide Prevention Curriculum — Goals and Objectives for Grades K–12

Unit	K	Grade 1	Grade 2	Grade 3	Grade 4	Grade 5
Self-Esteem	Recognizing the influence of others	Recognizing and explaining positive behavior	• Understand consequences • Importance of self to others	• Friendship development • Differences in self and others	Health and self-esteem	How personal qualities influence self-image
Feelings and Emotions	Recognizing feelings	• Identifying emotions • Group membership and emotions	• Recognizing pleasant and unpleasant emotions • Behavioral consequences	Differentiate between helpful and harmful behavior	• Use of communication • Emotions and decision-making	• Behavioral motivation • Emotional needs throughout life
Coping	Coping with hurt and upset feelings	Recognizing abilities and limits	Sharing feelings of loss	• Personal loss • Pleasant and unpleasant stress	Support systems	Effective and ineffective coping behavior
Locating and Giving Help	Helping resources	Whom to ask for help	Friends as helpers	Helping a friend	• Peer groups • Asking for help	Effect of peers on behavior
Suicide and Depression						
Life Plan						

158

Grade 6	Grade 7	Grade 8	Grade 9	Grade 10	Grade 11	Grade 12
Develop self-esteem by helping others	Enhancing self-esteem	Enhancing self-esteem	Enhancing self-esteem	Developing internal resources	Developing internal resources	Developing internal resources
• Managing feelings • Roles of significant others	Depression and suicide	Depression and suicide	Depression and suicide	Emotional health and behaviors that contribute to it	Emotional health and behaviors that contribute to it	Emotional health and behaviors that contribute to it
• Decision-making • Using the support system	Stress management	Stress management	Stress management	• Social well-being • Communication skills	• Social well-being • Communication skills	• Social well-being • Communication skills
• Effect of change • Adapting to change	• School, community resources • Self-help	• School, community resources • Self-help	• School, community resources • Self-help	Seeking and giving help	• Seeking and giving help • Community service	• Seeking and giving help • Community service
• Problem-solving process • Suicide • Getting help	• Problem-solving process • Suicide • Getting help	• Problem-solving process • Suicide • Getting help	• Suicide warning signs • Getting help	• Suicide • Referral • Being friend to oneself	• Suicide • Referral • Being friend to oneself	• Suicide • Referral • Being friend to oneself
					Personal mental health plan	Personal mental health plan

159

KINDERGARTEN — SELF-ESTEEM

Objectives:

• Students will recognize how others influence their feelings.
• Students will describe how helping others makes them feel good.

Activities:

1. Have students bring old magazines to class from which to cut pictures. Have students cut out pictures that show people doing "happy" or "fun" things and "unhappy" or "sad" things. Place a box with "Smiley Face" stickers in it on a table and a box with "Frowning Face" stickers next to it. Have each student put either a smiling or a frowning sticker on each of their pictures. Have each student explain why they selected a smile sticker for one of their pictures. Do the same for the "frown" sticker on each child's picture.
2. Have students cut one or two pictures from an old magazine showing an activity they enjoy doing at home or at school. Have the students tell the class why they enjoy the activity.
3. Have the students draw a picture of something they can do to help their parent(s), or other responsible adult. Have the students explain their picture to the class.

Every child in the class who wishes to share his or her pictures with the class should be given an opportunity. Since this might take a great deal of time, you may wish to do these activities in several class periods as a part of other regular class activities.

Suggested Readings for Class:

Borstein, Ruth. *Little Gorilla*. Boston: Seabury Press, Inc., 1976.
Brown, Marc T. *Arthur's Nose*. Boston: Little, Brown and Co., 1976.
Friskey, Margaret R. *Rackety, That Very Special Rabbit*. Chicago: Childrens Press, Inc., 1975.
Williams, Barbara W. *Someday, Said Mitchell*. New York: E. P. Dutton & Co., 1976.

FIRST GRADE — SELF-ESTEEM

Objectives:

- Students will name and describe different groups to which they belong, such as church groups, teams, clubs, and the YMCA-YWCA.
- Students will describe group activities that they enjoy and tell why they enjoy those activities.
- Students will be able to explain what behaviors are appropriate in a given group and those which are not appropriate.
- Students will be able to identify three positive qualities in themselves and two other persons (one should be an adult and one should be another student).

Activities:

1. Have the students, as a group, list the groups to which they belong. As they are listing them write them on the board or on a flip chart. When they have completed the list (every student should contribute the name of at least one group or should be a member of at least one group), ask the students to pick one group and draw a picture of what they do in that group. Ask the students to label the activity with a one- or two-sentence description. Share the pictures and descriptions with the class. After sharing, have the students make a bulletin board of their pictures; title the board appropriately.
2. Have students draw pictures of somebody behaving appropriately in one of the groups to which they belong. Then have the students draw a picture of somebody behaving inappropriately in one of the groups to which they belong. Lead a class discussion of the activity.
3. Have students, as a class, list what they think are positive qualities in a person. Students may describe an acceptable action rather than a quality. Each action or quality should be listed on the chalkboard or flip chart. Instruct the students to select three of the qualities or actions from the list written on the board or flip chart that they think best describes them. Have the students write those qualities down by completing the sentence, "I am special because. . . ."
4. Have each student name two people they admire, one a peer and one an adult. Each student should then draw a picture of each

individual they have chosen or obtain a photo of those individuals. Instruct the students to glue these pictures to the top of individual sheets of paper and to write down three actions or qualities from the class list that best describes the individuals. After this activity has been completed have the class make a bulletin board of their work. The students may also make a booklet of their work to eventually send home to parents as examples of class work.

Emphasize in class discussions the positive feelings the qualities and actions from the class list produce in students and others. Remind students of how these qualities and actions affect their behavior and how others react to them. Although the lesson did not include a discussion about negative qualities and actions, a limited number of negative examples can be used to illustrate that such qualities and behaviors can lead to unpleasant or unhappy consequences. Use appropriate judgment to decide whether or how much to deal with the negative.

Suggested Readings for Class:

Borstein, Ruth. *Little Gorilla*. Boston: Seabury Press, Inc., 1976.

Brown, Marc T. *Arthur's Nose*. Boston: Little, Brown and Co., 1976.

Friskey, Margaret R. *Rackety, That Very Special Rabbit*. Chicago: Childrens Press, Inc., 1975.

Mack, Nancy. *Why Me?* Milwaukee: Raintree Publishers, Ltd., 1976.

Stevens, Carla M. *Pig and the Blue Flag*. Boston: The Seabury Press, 1977.

Williams, Barbara W. *Someday, Said Mitchell*. New York: E. P. Dutton & Co., 1976.

SECOND GRADE — SELF-ESTEEM

Objectives:

- The students will understand that their behavior has consequences.
- The students will be able to describe why they are important to their family, friends, and the community.

Activities:

1. Have the students describe, as a group, all the things they can think of that families do with and for each other.

    Note: Take care to discuss the different kinds of families, such as two-parent, one-parent, foster, non-parent relative families, and even "families" that individuals put together who are not related at all in the usual manner. All these forms of family are "good" if they meet the needs of the individual. The important concept is for students to understand that they can receive support from such family groups.

2. Based on the discussion in Activity 1, have the students think of a helpful activity they do that makes someone else in their family feel good. Have them complete the sentence, "I make my family feel good by. . . ." Make a large scrapbook of all the things that the members of the class have written down in conjunction with pictures that students cut out of magazines or drew. Start a display in the classroom of pictures or objects the class brings in for a "Show and Tell" session each week on "Things We Do for Our Families." Place the class scrapbook in the center of the display.

    As the display grows, comment on how many different things people do for others and how it makes others feel. Point out that others and more likely to do things that make the students feel good when the students do things that make others feel good. Take the lead with the children, using the display to illustrate how this principle works in daily life.

3. Have the students list three behaviors for which they get rewarded and three behaviors for which they are not rewarded. Lead a class discussion to illustrate why people are rewarded or punished for different behaviors. Stress that because certain behavior results in punishment, or at least is not rewarded, does not mean that the student is bad. Point out that sometimes "bad" behavior is something that everybody does occasionally, but that it makes people

feel bad if others are hurt by that behavior. Tell the students that when they feel bad about something they've done, the best thing is to say they're sorry and then not dwell on the incident.

Resources:

- old magazines, scissors, glue, pictures of individuals selected by individual students
- small table for class display; colorful paper to decorate display

Suggested Readings for Class:

Carle, Eric. *The Mixed-Up Chameleon.* New York: Thomas Y. Crowell Company, Inc., 1975.

Christopher, Matthew F. *Glue Fingers.* Boston: Little, Brown and Company, 1975.

Mack, Nancy. *Why Me?* Milwaukee: Raintree Publishers, Ltd., 1976.

Meddaugh, Susan. *Too Short Fred.* Boston: Houghton Mifflin Company, 1978.

Stevens, Carla M. *Pig and the Blue Flag.* Boston: The Seabury Press, 1977.

Udry, Janice M. *How I Faded Away.* Chicago: Albert Whiteman & Company, 1976.

THIRD GRADE — SELF-ESTEEM

Objectives:

• Students will develop skills and behaviors that will enhance group membership and help develop friendships.
• Students will learn to recognize differences in themselves and others and should understand that "being different" is OK.
• Students will identify qualities or behaviors in themselves and others that enhance or detract from the image they have of themselves or that others have of themselves.

Activities:

1. Divide class into groups of five or six individuals. Give them all a common task such as creating a poster about drug and alcohol abuse, vandalism, smoking, or school spirit. Have each group decide what their poster will be about, what it will say, and the kind of picture that will be on it. Tell each group they must select specific people to do specific tasks. The groups should decide on the specific tasks, which should include drawing a rough draft of the poster, gathering information about the topic, and finding or drawing pictures that can be used on the poster. Other tasks the group might consider necessary are acceptable as long as the group performs the above three mandatory tasks. Instruct the groups that they should prepare the poster for display in two weeks; at that time the posters will be displayed in the classroom.

   Note: Perhaps have another teacher or the principal look at the posters and select one or more for display somewhere outside of the classroom. Area businesses may possibly display them in their windows. Also make positive comments on the efforts of each group and perhaps plan an appropriate reward for the entire class. The style of teaching and the nature of the class will determine what is most appropriate in this regard.

2. Declare a special week for "celebrating differences." You may wish to designate each day of the week as an opportunity to explore some area of difference. Racial, cultural, physical, intellectual, and personality differences are examples of "days" you could schedule. You can encourage students to bring in costumes or objects representing all the differences; this will add excitement to the class. *Pay particular attention to those groups and*

individuals who differ from the norm or the majority; the class can discuss and understand that the norm or the majority is not the only desirable model. Racial minorities and people with handicapping conditions are examples of these groups and individuals.

3. Provide all the students with the poem entitled "Why I Like My Friends" and have them underline or circle the qualities that they feel makes a good friend. After discussing their answers, ask them to add other qualities which make for good or bad friends. Have the students decide if a particular item is a characteristic of a good or bad friend.

   Note: The items in this poem are not all positive or negative; they can often be interpreted either way. Some may be items that students need to learn to handle since individuals may have little or no control over such characteristics. Introduce the concept of toleration of others as an integral part of this lesson through class discussion.

Why I Like My Friends

MY FRIENDS
are friendly most of the time
smile a lot
seldom laugh
listen to me when I want to talk about something important to me
buy me things
talk too much
are strong
steal things
take their turn but don't push ahead of others
are kind
are smart
are unfriendly
don't smile a lot
laugh a lot
are funny looking
are crabby
cheat
have a nice house
are dirty and smelly
are good looking
work hard
talk too loud
are good sports players

Resources:

* poster boards
* paints, magic markers, crayons, etc.
* enough copies of the "Why I Like My Friend" list for each student

Suggested Readings for Class:

Carle, Eric. *The Mixed-Up Chameleon.* New York: Thomas Y. Crowell Company, Inc., 1975.

Christopher, Matthew F. *Glue Fingers.* Boston: Little, Brown and Company, 1975.

Little, Jean. *Stand in the Wind.* New York: Harper & Row Publishers, Inc., 1975.

Mack, Nancy. *Why Me?* Milwaukee: Raintree Publishers, Ltd., 1976.

Meddaugh, Susan. *Too Short Fred.* Boston: Houghton Mifflin Company, 1978.

Stevens, Carla M. *Pig and the Blue Flag.* Boston: The Seabury Press, 1977.

Taylor, Paula. *Johnny Cash.* Mankato, MN: Creative Education, 1975.

Udry, Janice M. *How I Faded Away.* Chicago: Albert Whiteman & Company, 1976.

Wilkinson, Brenda S. *Ludell.* New York: Harper & Row Publishers, Inc., 1975.

FOURTH GRADE — SELF-ESTEEM

Objectives:

*   Students will understand the relationship between personal health and self-esteem.
*   Students will be able to list at least three ways in which they can influence how they feel about themselves.

Activities:

1. Have the class read the chapters in your school's health text that deal with exercise and nutrition. Discuss these chapters and have the students each make a "Good Health" chart listing good nutrition and exercise habits. Stress that good nutrition provides the fuel for exercise and for all the other work the body does.
2. Have a health professional visit the class and describe the emotional stress of poor health and illness. Have the guest discuss the positive emotional benefits of good health based on good nutrition and exercise. Obtain pamphlets from the county or city public health nurse that deal with this topic and hand them out to each student.
3. Have each student establish a plan to improve individual nutrition and exercise habits. The plans should include an intention to eat less candy, eat regularly, not skip meals, walk or run a certain distance regularly, and participate in active games or sports. Have the students use the forms, *My Health Plan* and the *Daily Health Plan Record*, to guide them with their plan. Have each student keep a record of how well he or she adheres to the plan and how he or she feels. Most of these students will be in good health and may not experience a great deal of difference, but even these students should be able to recognize a change in the way they feel after healthy exercise or eating. Stress how important it is for the students to plan throughout their lives to maintain health and emotional well-being.

    Note: Have each student turn in the *Health Plan Record* daily; keep the records in individual folders for one week. At the end of one week hand the folders back to the students and discuss their experience with them. Since most will not easily recognize the nutrition-exercise-feeling good relationship, emphasize it once again and make the point that people feel best about themselves when they feel good physically. Although the students were not asked to record their sleeping habits, you may want to bring up this topic in the discussion. If someone "lost" sleep during the week, you will be able to point out the physical and the emotional effects of loss of sleep, such as crabbiness.

My Health Plan

Name: _____

Address: _____

Date: _____

Foods I Eat New: _____

Foods I Will Eat Less Of: _____

Foods I Will Eat More Of: _____

Exercise I Get Now: _____

Exercise I Will Get Daily:_____

I Promise Myself I Will:
* Eat three meals each day.
* Not skip breakfast or any other meal.
* Eat the right foods each day.
* Get regular exercise every day.

Daily Health Plan Record

Name: _____

Date: _____

Things I Ate Today: _____

	Breakfast	Lunch	Dinner
1.			
2.			
3.			
4.			
5.			
6.			

Did I Follow My Plan?   Yes [ ]   No [ ]

Exercise I Did Today:

1. _____

2. _____

3. _____

4. _____

5. _____

Did I Follow My Plan Today?   Yes [ ]   No [ ]

How Do I Feel Today?
        Not So Good [ ]   Fair [ ]   Good [ ]   Very Good [ ]

Write Down Why You Circled The Answer Above:

_____

_____

_____

_____

_____

Suggested Readings for Class:

Herman, Charlotte. *The Difference of Ari Stein.* New York: Harper & Row Publishers, Inc., 1976.

Little, Jean. *Stand in the Wind.* New York: Harper & Row Publishers, Inc., 1975.

Mack, Nancy. *Why Me?* Milwaukee: Raintree Publishers, Ltd., 1976.

Neigoff, Mike. *Runner-Up.* Chicago: Albert Whiteman & Company, 1975.

Pevsner, Stella. *Keep Stompin' Till the Music Stops.* Boston: The Seabury Press, 1977.

Smith, Doris B. *Kelly's Creek.* New York: Thomas Y. Crowell Company, Inc., 1975.

Stevens, Carla M. *Pig and the Blue Flag.* Boston: The Seabury Press, 1977.

Taylor, Paula. *Johnny Cash.* Mankato, MN: Creative Education, 1975.

Wilkinson, Brenda S. *Ludell.* New York: Harper & Row Publishers, Inc., 1975.

FIFTH GRADE — SELF-ESTEEM

Objectives:

- Students will identify and value their own personal qualities and the qualities of others.
- Students will recognize how their self-image is influenced by their personal qualities and abilities.

Activities:

1. Have the students keep a diary for one week in which they record each positive ting they do for themselves or others. They should record things such as favors they did for someone, helping someone with a task, saying something ice, and some enjoyable activity they did. The students should try to record this on a daily basis at the end of one day or the beginning of the next. At the end of the week, have the students read the diary to themselves and write a short paragraph describing what they like about themselves. Without revealing the identity of the authors, read and discuss several of the paragraphs. Point out to the class that each student has many positive qualities and each should be appreciated by himself and herself and others.
2. Have the students keep a second diary in which they observe and record positive things others do to help friends. At the end of one week have the students present their findings to the rest of the class. Discuss with them what they have recorded. Ask them then to pick one of the people they wrote about and describe what kind of a person would do the things that individual did.
3. Ask each student to write about five things they like to do and five things they like about themselves. Discuss why people enjoy doing things well, emphasizing that people do things well because they are born with some skills that are stronger than others. Discuss with the class why they define themselves as good students, good athletes, or good chess players, for example. Tell them that each of them is born with many skills and they can choose to develop any of them. Point out to them that an individual who cannot do something well should not feel that he or she is a lesser person because of it; each person can do some things better than others can. Tell the students that one of the most interesting parts of life is finding out what they can do well and trying to enjoy those things fully.

Also, tell them that school provides one place or them to try many things so they can discover what they can do and enjoy.

Suggested Readings for Class:

Herman, Charlotte. *The Difference of Ari Stein.* New York: Harper & Row Publishers, Inc., 1976.

Little, Jean. *Stand in the Wind.* New York: Harper & Row Publishers, Inc., 1975.

Neigoff, Mike. *Runner-Up.* Chicago: Albert Whiteman & Company, 1975.

Pevsner, Stella. *Keep Stompin' Till the Music Stops.* Boston: The Seabury Press, 1977.

Smith, Doris B. *Kelly's Creek.* New York: Thomas Y. Crowell Company, Inc., 1975.

Stevens, Carla M. *Pig and the Blue Flag.* Boston: The Seabury Press, 1977.

Taylor, Paula. *Johnny Cash.* Mankato, MN: Creative Education, 1975.

Wilkinson, Brenda S. *Ludell.* New York: Harper & Row Publishers, Inc., 1975.

Media Resource:

Liking Me: Building Self-Esteem. Filmstrip or videocassette, 1988. Sunburst Communications, 101 Castleton Street, Pleasantville, New York 10570-9971.

SIXTH GRADE — SELF-ESTEEM

Objectives:

- Students will learn that helping others is one way to feel good about themselves.
- Students will learn by observation how their actions can make someone else feel good.

Activities:

1. Take the class on a field trip to a nursing home or to the pediatric ward at a hospital. Have the class sing or present some other program to the patients. Encourage the students to talk to individual patients about topics both feel comfortable discussing.
2. Have the class select a special service project; help them plan how to accomplish it, then carry it out. Have each student write a short description of what the project achieved and how doing it made them feel.

   Note: These activities will require that you clear your project with school administration and make appropriate arrangements with the administration of any institution you plan to visit or work with. Parental permission for student participation is also required. Handling these tasks and other logistical problems that might arise are worth the effort to give the students this kind of experience.

Suggested Readings for Class:

Bailey, Pearle. *Duey's Tale*. New York: Harcourt Brace Jovanovich, Inc., 1975.

Herman, Charlotte. *The Difference of Ari Stein*. New York: Harper & Row Publishers, Inc., 1976.

Lampman, Evelyn S. *The Potlatch Family*. New York: Atheneum Publishers, 1976.

Little, Jean. *Stand in the Wind*. New York: Harper & Row Publishers, Inc., 1975.

Neigoff, Mike. *Runner-Up*. Chicago: Albert Whiteman & Company, 1975.

Pevsner, Stella. *Keep Stompin' Till the Music Stops*. Boston: The Seabury Press, 1977.

Pfeffer, Susan B. *Marly the Kid*. New York: Doubleday & Company, Inc., 1975.

Smith, Doris B. *Kelly's Creek*. New York: Thomas Y. Crowell Company, Inc., 1975.

Stevens, Carla M. *Pig and the Blue Flag*. Boston: The Seabury Press, 1977.

Taylor, Paula. *Johnny Cash*. Mankato, MN: Creative Education, 1975.

Wilkinson, Brenda S. *Ludell and Willie*. New York: Harper & Row Publishers, Inc., 1978.

Wilkinson, Brenda S. *Ludell*. New York: Harper & Row Publishers, Inc., 1975.

Appendix D: Postvention Guides

LEGAL AND ADMINISTRATIVE ISSUES

Sample Emergency Procedures
School Response for Dealing with Tragic Death or Attempted Suicide

The death, suicide, or attempted suicide of a student, faculty member, or alumnus *may* precipitate the need for a school response.

Preparation for the Emergency

The school district will have a phone tree in place to notify staff *before* arrival at school.

The school district will have provided inservice training to *all* staff on prevention, intervention, and postvention techniques. Once initial training has taken place, each fall, new faculty and staff will be brought up to date with this information.

The school district will have selected the members of the Crisis Team (suggested: counselors, school psychologist, superintendent).

The school district will have provided Crisis Team members and any other staff members identified as being available as counselors during the crisis with up-to-date training.

Legal and administrative issues taken from Deaton, Bob, and Dan Morgan. 1992. *Managing Death Issues in the School.* Monograph No. 1, Appendix A. Montana Office of Public Instruction, Helena, MT.

The school district will have an agreement with the Valley Consortium of Counselors (or other outside agency, if desired) to provide mutual assistance during the crisis.

The school district will have identified a "safe" room for exclusive use during the crisis.

Death, Suicide, or Attempted Suicide Reported

Notified party informs superintendent/principal.
Telephone tree informs all staff members.
Extra counselors are called in.

First Day

A. Morning faculty/staff meeting at 7:30 A.M. Staff reminded of their training and given information on the incident and a written announcement to be read to the first class of the day.
B. Media contacts are handled by Crisis Team designee (most likely the administrative representative on the team).
C. Safe Room made available to students and staff, provided all day.
D. A counselor will go to each class and activity the student usually participated in to share feelings and answer questions. Counselors will also attend other classes as needed or requested.
E. Crisis Team member will contact family about funeral arrangements, memorial service, etc.
F. Counselors will take referrals from staff, parents, students, and self-referrals.
G. After school faculty/staff meeting at 3:10 P.M. Review and staff support; Crisis Team gets referrals on high risk students.

Second Day

A. Announcement from the Crisis Team administrator on funeral, memorial arrangements.
B. Students and staff encouraged to attend.
C. Safe Room still available for students.
D. Crisis Team provides assistance to family if needed.
E. After-school faculty/staff meeting. Continue monitoring high risk students. Continue staff support.
F. Crisis Team will consider large group gathering to help other students process their feelings. Not all students will come forward or have someone identify their needs.
G. A formal critical incident debriefing will be scheduled within three days if it is determined in (E) after school faculty/staff meeting that it is needed.

"TAKING CARE OF THOSE WHO TAKE CARE"
A DEBRIEFING GUIDE FOR SCHOOL MEMBERS

Following any tragic death of a school member, teachers, staff and administrators need to share thought and feelings and reach a sense of closure about the event. The critical incident debriefing is a planned, thoughtful way to provide for the needs of staff and acknowledge the loss of the person who died.

Formal debriefing utilizing a trained debriefing team, should be considered, especially if everyone on the school staff was affected by the incident, or if no one is available to facilitate from the school.

When should it be held: 24–72 hours after the news of the death is optimum.

Who should attend: All school staff who feel directly affected by the death of a fellow teacher, staff member, or student.

What is a debriefing like:

1. Setting and time — A private conference room where people can be seated around a large table for about two hours is best.
2. Ground rules — Free expression is encouraged and everything said is confidential. The focus is upon the personal expression of those attending. It is not an administrative critique or investigation in any sense.
3. Expression and exchange — Each person is given the opportunity to talk about his/her relationship to the deceased and how they feel affected by the incident. Next cognitive work is done by members as they make sense and make peace with themselves through exchanging thoughts about the life and death of this person.
4. Stress management instruction (optional) — Some debriefing sessions end with suggesting specific techniques for self-care in dealing with stresses related with a tragic incident. These include sleep disturbance, nutrition and exercise, and dealing with intrusive mental images.

GUIDELINES FOR ACTION FOLLOWING
THE DEATH OF A CHILD AND ADOLESCENT

Postvention Efforts for Counselors and Therapists:

1. Consider location. Some parents and families may need to be seen in their own homes rather than the therapist's office.
2. Anticipate anger. If there has been therapy prior to the death, there may be anger toward the therapist or the therapy process.
3. Encourage any expression of feelings. While it is the most obvious measure, family members often receive signals from others that they do not

want to hear about the child's death because of their own uncomfortableness. The counselor needs to invite the family or parents to say what they need to say.

4. Immediate cognitive issues. Be alert for family members' request to make sense of the tragedy, and be clear about the need to work through thoughts and ideas *in addition to feelings*. Typical cognitive issues are: "What else could I/we have done to save him? It's all my fault she died. What will people say about the suicide? He doesn't seem to be really gone. I can't stand to think of all we invested in her, and now she's gone forever."

5. Spiritual issues. Suicides and other tragic deaths involve the core value about the meaning and value of life to the person. Saving people from suicide involves appealing to their personal beliefs about life being worthwhile. The aftermath is often difficult for people who have not separated their religiousness from spiritualness. A competent clergyman should deal with spirituality where appropriate.

6. Practical issues. Assist the family in planning what they would like to do with the deceased's belonging, his room, car, etc. Discuss memorial services and contributions. Help the family sort out the difference between what they truly want and what they perceive others want from them. Remind parents that serious marital conflict often erupts after a tragic child death in the family. Appeal to them to work together. Offer to help them later as needed.

7. Closure. Assist the family with moving along in the grief and letting go processes. Since closure varies greatly among different people, note signs of getting "stuck" and not moving along.

Prepared by Bob Deaton, Professor,
Department of Social Work, University of Montana

References

American Association of Suicidology. (1987). Proceedings of the Annual Conference, Denver, CO.

American Association of Suicidology. (1981). *Suicide prevention training manual.* West Point, NY: Merck, Sharp, and Dohme.

American Psychiatric Association. (1987). *Diagnostic and statistical manual of mental disorders.* Washington, DC: American Psychiatric Association.

American Psychological Association. (1989). Ethical principles of psychologists. *American Psychologists, 45,* pp. 390–395.

Anthony, E. J., & Cohker, B. (Eds.). (1987). *The invulnerable child.* New York: Guilford.

Behaviors related to unintentional and intentional injuries among high school students — United States. (1991). *Journal of School Health, 62,* (9), 439–443.

Benard, B. (1991). *Fostering resiliency in kids: Protective factors in the family, school and community.* Portland, OR: Western Center for Drug Free Schools and Communities.

Bennett, L., Wolin, S., & Reiss, D. (1988). Cognitive, behavioral, and emotional problems among school-age children of alcoholic parents. *American Journal of Psychiatry 145* (2), 185-190.

Berkan, W. A. (1990). *Suicide Prevention: Guide to Curricular Planning in Suicide Prevention.* Madison, WI: Wisconsin Department of Public Instruction.

Berkan, W. A. (1986). *Suicide prevention: A resource and planning guide.* Madison, WI: Wisconsin Department of Public Instruction.

Berman, A. L. (1991). Suicide intervention in schools: Critical reflections. In A. A. Leenaars and S. Wenckstern (Eds.), *Suicide prevention in schools.* New York, NY: Hemisphere.

Berman, A. L. *Suicide prevention: Case consultations.* New York: Springer.

Berman, A. L., & Jobes, D. (1991). *Adolescent suicide: Assessment and intervention.* Washington, DC: American Psychological Association.

Berndt, T., & Ladd, G. (1989). *Peer relationships in child development.* New York: John Wiley and Sons.

Bernstein, J. E., & Gullo, S. V. (1977). *When people die.* New York: E. P. Dutton.

Blum, Robert, Harmon, B., Harris, L., Bergeisen, L., & Resnick, M. (1992). American Indian-Alaska Native Youth Health. *Journal of the American Medical Association, 267* (12), 1637–1644.

Blumenthal, S. J., & Kupfer, D. J. (1988). Overview of early detection and treatment strategies for suicidal behavior in young people. *Journal of Youth and Adolescence, 17* (1), 1–23.

Bongar, B. (1991). *The suicidal patient: Clinical and legal standards of care.* Washington, DC: American Psychological Association.

Bowers, G., Pekarske, M., Wiese, B., Knorr, J., Johnson, J. D., Muir, C., Paul, S., Price, J., & Zwickey, J. (1988). *Suicide prevention curriculum.* Appleton, WI: Appleton Area School District.

Bradley, C. (1987). *A guide to curriculum planning in health education.* Madison, WI: Wisconsin Department of Public Instruction.

Brooks, J., Nomura, C., & Cohen, P. (1989). A network of influences on adolescent drug involvement: neighborhood, school, peer, and family. *Genetic, Social and General Psychology Monographs 115* (1), 303–321.

California State Department of Education. (1990). *Toward a state of esteem: The final report of the California task-force to promote self-esteem and personal and social responsibility.* Sacramento, CA: California State Department of Education.

Carnegie Corporation of New York. (1992). *A matter of time, risk and opportunity in the nonschool hours.* Report of the Task Force on Youth Development and Community Programs. New York: Carnegie Corporation of New York.

Carrol, D. (1985). *Living with the dying.* New York: McGraw-Hill.

Centers for Disease Control and Prevention. (1993). *The prevention of youth violence: A framework for community action.* Atlanta, GA: Centers for Disease Control and Prevention.

Chance, S. (1992). *Stronger than death: When suicide touches your life.* New York: W.W. Norton.

Chess, S. (1989). Defying the voice of doom. In T. Dugan and Robert Coles (Eds.), *The child in our times.* New York: Brunner-Mazel.

Clark, R. (1983). *Family life and school achievement: Why poor black children succeed or fail.* Chicago, IL: University of Chicago Press.

Claymore, B. J. (1988). A public health approach to suicide attempts on a Sioux reservation. *American Indian and Alaska Native Mental Health Research, 1* (3), 19–24.

Coleman, J. (1987). Families and schools. *Educational Researcher, 16* (6), 32–38.

Coombs, J. (1990). *Study on suicide.* New York: Mental Health Materials Center.

Corr, C. A., & McNeil, J. N. (1986). *Adolescence and death.* New York: Springer.

Cowen, E., et al. (1990). Relationships between support and adjustment among children of divorce. *Journal of Child Psychology and Psychiatry 31* (5), 727–735.

Curran, D. K. (1987). *Adolescent Suicidal Behavior.* New York: Hemisphere.

Davidson, L., Linnoila, M. (1991). *Risk factors for youth suicide*. New York: Hemisphere.

Deaton, R. L. (1991). Can suicide be prevented, and should we try? Unpublished paper, presented at Third Annual Youth in Crisis Conference, Great Falls, MT.

Deaton, R. L., & Morgan, D. (1992). *Managing death issues in the schools*. Monograph no. 1. Helena, MT: Montana Office of Public Instruction.

____. (1990). Intervention handout packet on teen suicide. Missoula, MT: University of Montana, Department of Social Work.

Demos, V. (1989). Resiliency in infancy. In T. Dugan and Robert Coles (Eds.), *The Child in Our Times* (pp. 3–22). New York: Brunner-Mazel

Dershimer, R. A. (1990). *Counseling the bereaved*. New York: Pergamon.

Elkind, D. (1981). *The hurried child: Growing up too fast too soon*. Redding, MA: Addison-Wesley.

Elkind, D. (1975). *A sympathetic understanding of the child: birth to sixteen*. Boston: Allyn and Bacon.

Erikson, E. H. (1968). *Identity, youth, and crisis*. New York: W.W. Norton.

____. (1963). *Childhood and society* (2nd ed.). New York: W.W. Norton.

Everstine D., & Everstine, L. (1993). *The trauma response*. New York: W.W. Norton.

Feldman, R., Stiffman, A., & Jung, K. (Eds.). (1987). *Children at risk: In the web of parental mental illness*. New Brunswick, NJ: Rutgers University Press.

Felsman, J. K. (1989). Risk and resiliency in childhood: The lives of street children. In T. Dugan and Robert Coles (Eds.), *The child in our times*. New York: Brunner-Mazel.

Figley, C. K. (1988). Post traumatic family therapy. In E. M. Ocherd (Ed.), *Post traumatic therapy and victims of violence*. New York: Brunner-Mazel.

Flandreau-West, M. (1988). *Protective behaviors*. Madison, WI: Wisconsin Committee for the Prevention of Child Abuse and Neglect.

Frymier, J. (1992). *Growing up is risky business, and schools are not to blame*. Bloomington, IN: Phi Delta Kappa.

Fullan, M. G., & Stiegelbauer, S. (1991). *The new meaning of educational change*. New York: Teachers College Press.

Galusha, R. (n.d.). *Omaha student suicide prevention and intervention programs*. Omaha, NE: Omaha Public Schools, Psychological Services.

Giffin, M., & Felsenthal, C. (1983). *A cry for help*. New York: Doubleday.

Gifford, B., & Cleary, B. (1990). Supporting the bereaved. *American Journal of Nursing, 20*, 142–147.

Glasser, W. (1990). *The quality school: Managing students without coercion*. New York: Harper & Row.

Goodstadt, M. S. (1974). Myths and methodology in drug education: A critical review of the research evidence. In M. S. Goodstadt (Ed.), *Research on methods and programs of drug education*. Toronto: Addiction Research Foundation.

Gordon, S. (1985). *When living hurts*. New York: Dell.

Grossberg, M. (1993). Children's Legal Rights? A Historical Look at a Legal Paradox. In R. Wollons (Ed.), *Children at risk in America* (pp. 113–118). Albany, NY: State University of New York Press.

Gunfire's tragic toll costs young lives — and money. (1993, November 26). *Missoulian* (Missoula, MT), C–4.

Hammer, M. D., Nichols, J., & Armstrong, L. (1992). A ritual of remembrance. *The American Journal of Maternal/Child Nursing, 17,* 310–313.

Harness-Overley, P. (1992). *A message of hope for surviving the tragedy of suicide.* Upland, CA: Bradley.

Hawkins, J. D., et al. (1985). Childhood predictors and the prevention of adolescent substance abuse. In *Etiology of Drug Abuse: Implications for Prevention.* NIDA Research Monograph 56. Rockville, MD: National Institute on Drug Abuse.

Hill, J. P. (1980). *Understanding early adolescence: A framework.* Chapel Hill, NC: University of North Carolina.

Hoff, Lee Ann. (1991). Crisis intervention in schools. In A. A. Leenaars and S. Wenckstern (Eds.), *Suicide prevention in schools.* New York, NY: Hemisphere.

Jackson, E. N. (1966). *Telling a child about death.* New York: Channel.

Jacobs, J. (1971). *Adolescent suicide.* New York: Irvington.

Johnson, K. (1993). *School crisis management.* Alameda, CA: Hunter House.

Kirk, W. G. (1993). *Adolescent suicide: A school based approach to assessment and intervention.* Champaign, IL: Research Press.

Kolehmainen, J., & Handwerk, S. (1986). *Teen suicide: A book for friends, family, and classmates.* Minneapolis, MN: Lerner.

Konopka, G., (1973). Requirements for healthy development of adolescent youth. *Adolescence, 8,* 291–316.

Kozol, J. (1991). *Savage inequalities.* New York: Crown.

Kurth-Schai, R. (1988). The roles of youth in society: A reconceptualization. *Educational Forum, 52* (2), 131-132.

Lawrence, M. T., & Ureda, J. R. (1990). Student recognition of and response to suicidal peers. *Suicide and Life Threatening Behavior, 20* (20), 164–176.

Leenaars, A., & Wenckstern, S. (1991). Posttraumatic stress disorder: A conceptual model for postvention. *Suicide prevention in schools.* New York: Hemisphere.

Levin, H. (1988). Accelerated schools for disadvantaged students. *Educational Leadership* 44 (6), 19-21.

Lipsitz, J. S. (1980). *Toward adolescence: The middle school years.* Chicago, IL: University of Chicago Press.

Lofquist, W. A. (1983). *Discovering the meaning of prevention.* Tucson, AZ: Associates for Youth Development.

Lucas, C. (1972). *Our western educational heritage.* New York: Macmillan.

Martens, R. (1978). *Joy and sadness in children's sports.* Champaign, IL: Human Kinetics Publishers.

Martens, R., & Seafeldt, V. (1979). *Guidelines for children's sports.* Reston, VA: The American Alliance for Health, Physical Education, Recreation and Dance.

McWhirter, J., Jeffries, J., Benedict, T., Anna M., & Ellen H. (1993). *At risk youth: A comprehensive response.* Pacific Grove, CA: Brooks-Cole.

Melaville, A., & Blank, M. (1993). *Together we can: A guide for crafting a profamily system of education and human services.* Washington, DC: U.S. Government Printing Office.

Miller, A., & Ohlin, L. (1985). *Delinquency and community: Creating opportunities and controls.* Newbury Park, CA: Sage.

Mitchell, J. (1983). When disaster strikes: the critical incident stress debriefing process. *Journal of Emergency Medicine, 8* (1), 36–39.

Mitchell, J., & Bray, G. (1990). *Emergency services stress.* Englewood Cliffs, NJ: Prentice-Hall.

Montana Department of Health and Environmental Sciences. (1990). *Montana Vital Statistics: 1988–1989.* Helena, MT.

Montana Office of Public Instruction. (1993). *Crisis Management in the schools.* Helena, MT: Southwest Regional Laboratories.

Nash, M. A. (1990). *Improving their chances: A handbook for designing and implementing programs for at-risk youth.* Madison, WI: University of Wisconsin at Madison, School of Education, Vocational Studies Center.

National Center for Injury Prevention and Control. (1993). *The prevention of youth violence: A framework for community action.* Atlanta, GA: Centers for Disease Control and Prevention.

Newcomb, M., & Bentler, P. (1986). Drug use, educational aspirations, and workforce involvement: The transition from adolescence to youth adulthood. *American Journal of Community Psychology, 14* (3), 303-321.

Ogden, E., & Germinario, V. (1988). *The at risk student.* Lancaster, PA: Technomic.

Palmo, A., et al. (1988). Development of a policy and procedures statement for crisis situations in the school. *The School Counselor, 36* (2), 94-102.

Parkman, S. E. (1992). Helping families say goodbye. *Journal of Maternal/Child Nursing, 17,* 14-17.

Patros, Philip G. & Shamoo, Tonia K. (1989). *Depression and suicide in children and adolescents.* Needham Heights, MA: Allyn and Bacon.

Peck, M., Farberow, N., & Litman, R. (1985). *Youth suicide.* New York: Springer.

Pfeffer, C. R. (1989). *Suicide among youth: perspectives on risk and prevention.* Washington, DC: American Psychiatric Press.

_____. (1986). *The suicidal child.* New York: Guilford Press.

Popple, P., & Leighninger, L. (1993). *Social work, social welfare, and American society.* Needham Heights, MA: Allyn and Bacon.

Robertson, J. D. (1988). *Psychiatric Malpractice: Liability of Mental Health Professionals.* New York: John Wiley.

Robertson, J. D., & Mathews, B. (1989). Preventing adolescent suicide with group counseling. *Journal of Specialists for Group Work, 14* (1), 34-39.

Ross, C. P. (1985). Teaching children the facts of life and death: Suicide prevention in the schools. In M. Peck (Ed.), *Youth suicide.* New York: Springer.

Rutter, M. (1984, March). Resilient children. *Psychology Today, 18* (3), 57-65.

Rutter, M. (1979). Protective factors in children's responses to stress and disadvantage. In M. W. Kent and J. E. Rolf (Eds.), *Primary prevention of psychopathology,* Vol. 3: *Social competence in children* (pp. 49-74). Hanover, NH: University Press of New England.

Rutter, M., Maughan, B., Mortimore, P., & Ouston, J. (1979). *Fifteen thousand hours.* Cambridge, MA: Harvard University Press.

Ryan-Wenger, N. (1992). A taxonomy of children's coping strategies: A step toward theory development. *American Journal of Orthopsychiatry, 62* (2), 256.

Sargent, Marilyn. (1989). *Depressive illnesses: Treatments bring hope.* Publication Number: 89-1491. Rockville, MD: U.S. Dept of Health and Human Services.

Seligman, M. (1975). *Helplessness: On depression, development, and death.* San Francisco, CA: Freeman.

Shafer, D., Garland, A., Gould, M., Fisher, P., & Trautman, P. (1988). Preventive teenage suicide: A critical review. *Journal of the American Academy of Child and Adolescent Psychiatry, 27* (6), 675–687.

Shorr, L. (1988). *Within our reach: breaking the cycle of disadvantage.* New York: Doubleday.

Simon, R. L. (1988). *Concise guide to clinical psychiatry and the law.* Washington, DC: American Psychiatric Press.

Slack, K. A. (1984). *Crisis intervention: A handbook for practice and research.* Boston, MA: Allyn & Bacon.

Spirito, A., Brown, L., Overholser, J., & Fritz, G. (1989). Attempted suicide in adolescence: A review and critique of the literature. *Clinical Psychology Review, 9,* 335–363.

U.S. Bureau of the Census. (1991). *Statistical Abstract of the United States* (pp. 78, 80, 82). Washington, DC: U.S. Bureau of the Census.

Tarasoff vs. Regents of the University of California. 2d 334, 131. (n.d.). *California Reporter.* 14. Cal Supreme Court. Sacremento, CA. p. 551.

Tierney, R., Ramsay, R., Tanny, B., & Lang, W. (1991). Comprehensive school suicide prevention programs. In A. A. Leenaars and S. Wenckstern (Eds.), *Suicide prevention in schools* (pp. 83–93). New York: Hemisphere.

Tugend, A. (1985). Suicide prevention: Programs and school liability. *Education Week, 5,* 12.

Villa, R. A., Thousand, J. S., Stainback, W., & Stainback, S. (1992). *Restructuring for caring and effective education.* Baltimore, MD: Paul H. Brookes.

Vital Records and Statistics Bureau. (1993). *Montana Vital Statistics, 1990–1991.* Helena, MT: State of Montana, Vital Records and Statistics Bureau.

Wallerstein, J., & Kelly, J. (1980). *Surviving the breakup.* New York: Basic Books.

Wass, H. (1983). *Death education in the home and school.* Springfield, VA: ERIC Document Reproduction Services.

Wehlage, G. G., Rutter, R. A., Smith, G. A., Lesko, N., & Fernandez, R. R. (1989). *Reducing the risk: Schools as communities of support.* Philadelphia, PA: The Palmer Press.

Weir, M. (1991). *The effect of the positive action program on the self esteem of sixth graders* (pp. 11–20). Ph.D. dissertation, University of Montana.

Weirs, M. R. (1989). Youth sports: Is winning everything? *Childhood Education, 66* (4), 195–196.

Werner, E. (1990). Protective factors and individual resilience. In S. Metsels and J. Shonkoff (Eds.), *Handbook of early childhood intervention.* New York: Cambridge University Press.

Werner, E., & Smith, R. (1982) *Vulnerable but invincible: A longitudinal study of resilient children and youth.* New York: Adams, Bannister, and Cox.

Wheatley, G. H. (1991). Constructivist perspective on science and mathematics learning. *Science Education, 75* (1), 9-12.

Williams, T., & Kornblum, W. (1985). *Growing up poor.* Lexington, MA: D.C. Heath.

Wisconsin, State of. (1985). Assembly Bill 180, Wisconsin Statutes 118.295. Madison, WI.

Wollons, Roberta (Ed.). (1993). *Children at risk in America.* Albany, NY: State University of New York Press.

Wrobleski, A. (1991). *Suicide survivors: A guide for those left behind*. Minneapolis, MN: Afterwards.

Zalaznik, P. (1992). *Dimensions of loss and death education*, 3rd ed. Minneapolis, MN: Edu-Pac.

Index

ABOUT THE AUTHORS

William A. Berkan is a school social work consultant in the Wisconsin Department of Public Instruction. He has published three monographs for the Wisconsin Department of Public Instruction on suicide prevention, child abuse, and neglect.

Robert L. Deaton is a professor of social work at the University of Montana and team leader of the Missoula Critical Incident Team. He coordinates a Critical Incident Team that responds to fatalities with emergency service staff and frequently assists area schools following a teen suicide. Professor Deaton co-authored a monograph on youth suicide prevention and intervention for the Montana Office of Public Instruction. He also does counseling and staff training in the field.

Daniel M. Morgan is a youth court officer and director of the intensive family counseling program for the Fourth Judicial District, Missoula, Montana. He co-authored Monograph No. One for the Montana Office of Public Instruction and has extensive experience counseling, consulting, and training staff in youth suicide.